Shrova Mall

A-to-Z e-commerce full-stack application

  stripe  shippo Firebase  git Render

Abdelfattah Ragab

Shrova Mall

A-to-Z e-commerce full-stack application

Abdelfattah Ragab

Source code

The source code is available on the book's website
https://books.abdelfattah-ragab.com

Introduction

Welcome to the book "Shrova Mall: A-to-Z e-commerce full-stack application". In this book, I explain how you can create a full-stack e-commerce application using Angular and NestJS.
The application provides payment and shipping functionalities by integrating Stripe for payments and Shippo for shipping.
To begin, I will show you the application we are going to build and then start by creating the database. Next, I will explain the backend and finally the frontend application. By the end of this book, you will be able to create your online e-commerce store and cover all possible scenarios.
Let's get started.

Screenshots

I will start by showing some screenshots of the application to understand what we are about to build.

The homepage

KUCCU Stand Food
Mixer, 6.5 Qt 660W

KitchenAid 5 Ultra Power
Speed Hand Mixer -
KHM512, Aqua Sky

CHEFMAN
Multifunctional Digital
Air Fryer

Nuwave Brio 15.5Qt Air
Fryer Rotisserie Oven

Emeril Lagasse (4-
00675-02) 26 QT

Nuwave Bravo Air Fryer
Toaster Smart Oven

Shintenchi 74"
Convertible Sectional
Sofa Couch

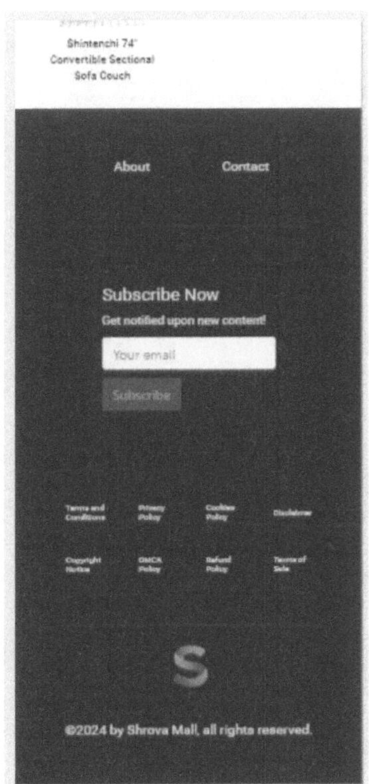

You should improve your styling and include more promotional staff on the homepage, but I'll leave that up to you.

The admin sidenav

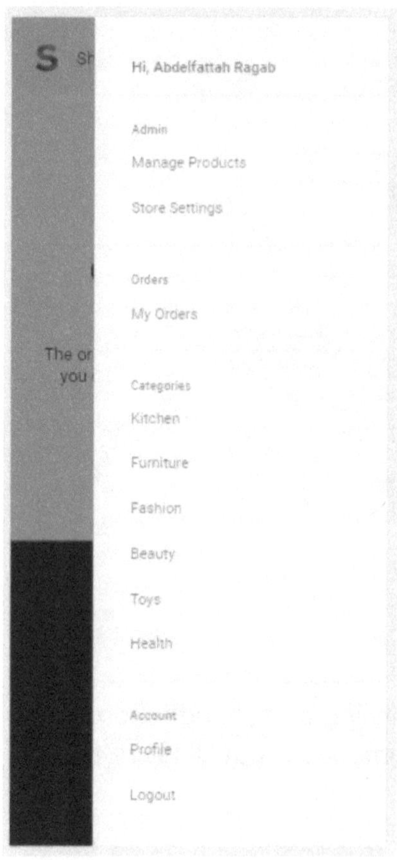

The manage products page

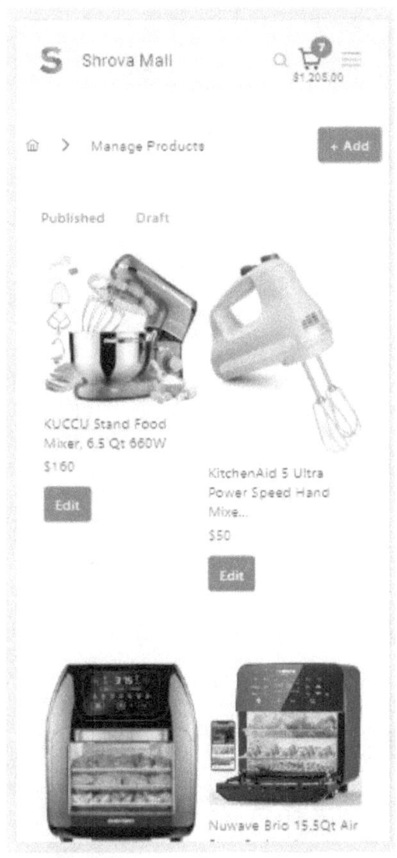

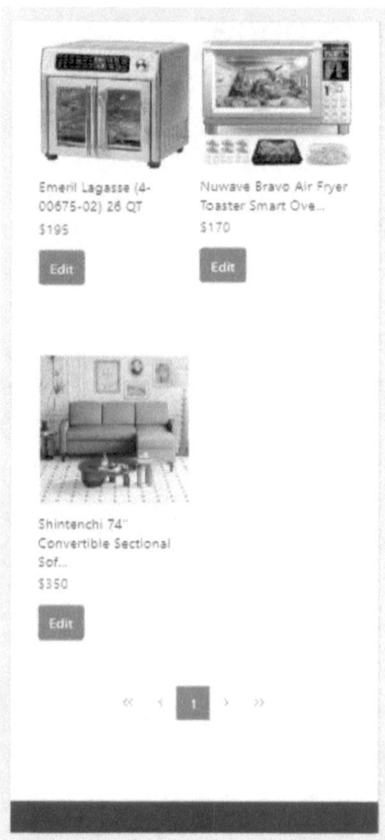

This page is only for administrators to manage products.

The add product page

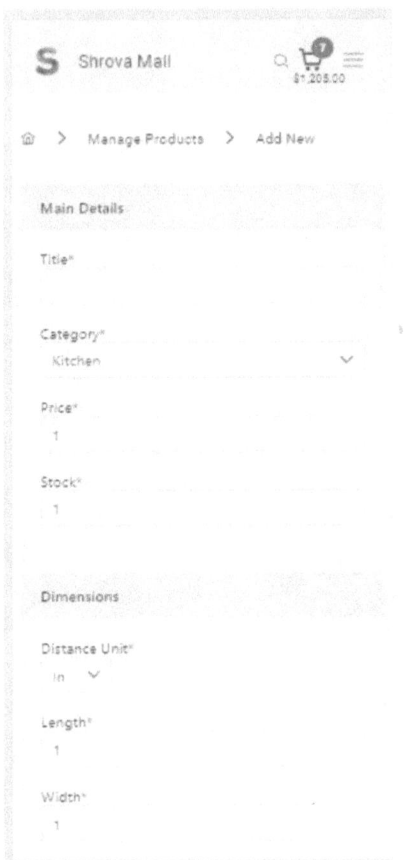

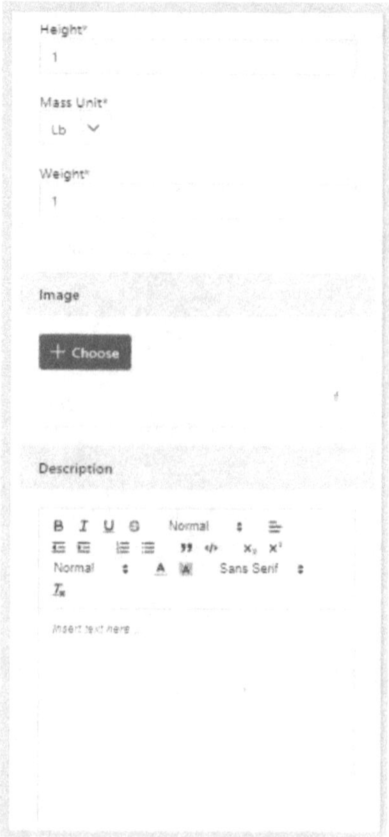

Height*
1
Mass Unit*
Lb
Weight*
1
Image
+ Choose
Description
B I U S Normal
Normal
Sans Serif
Insert text here ...

Save
Published
About
Contact
Subscribe Now
Get notified upon new content!
Your email
Subscribe

The store settings page

The store details are used as the shipping address when sending products to customers

The register page

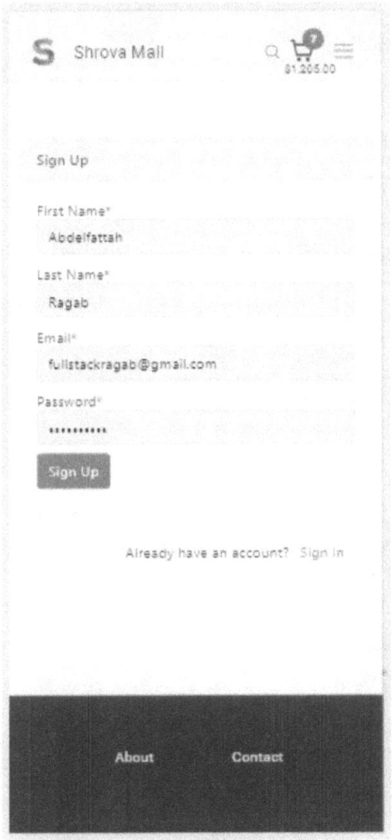

The login page

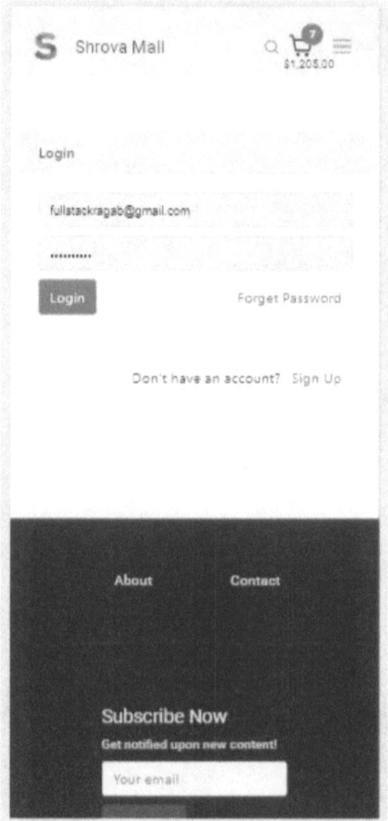

The forget password page

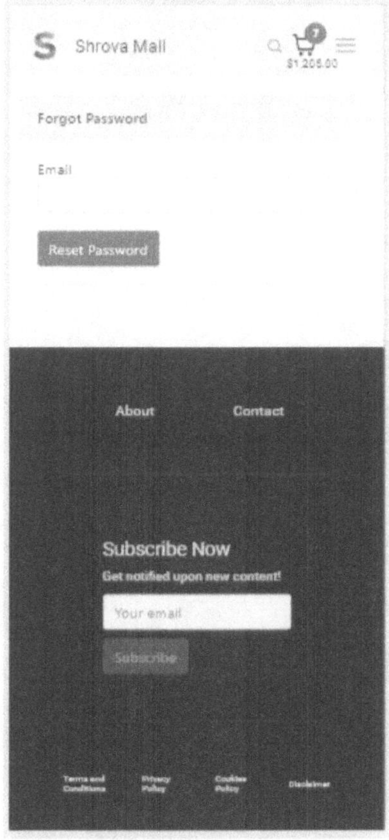

The reset password page

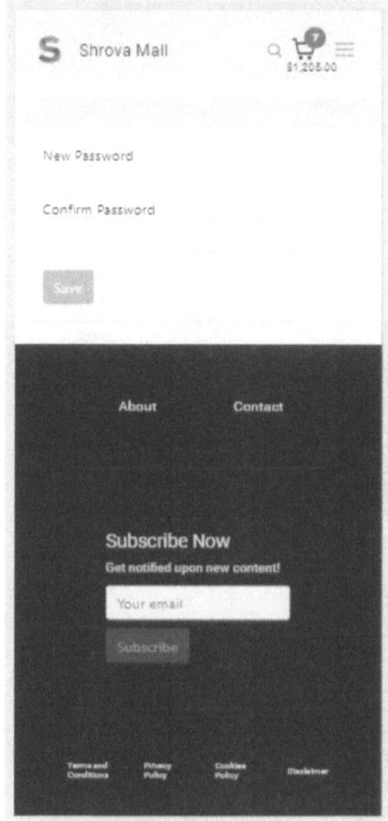

The about page

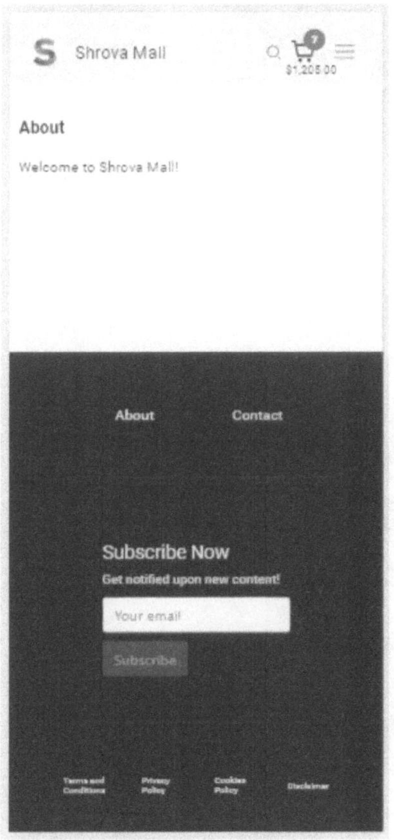

The contact page

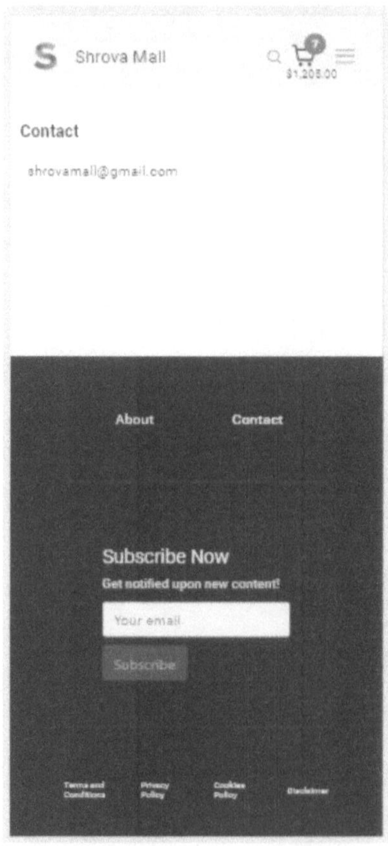

The policies pages

You should add policy pages for:
- cookies-policy
- copyright-notice
- disclaimer
- dmca-policy
- privacy-policy
- refund-policy

- terms-and-conditions
- terms-of-sale

Depending on your needs, you can add all or some of them.

The profile page

The profile/address page

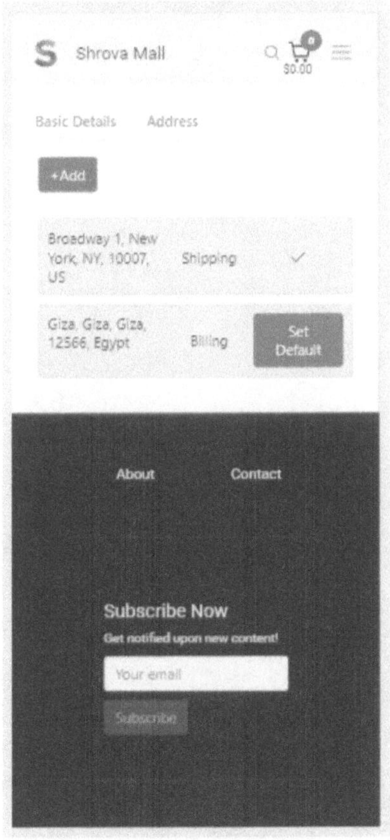

The profile/address add page

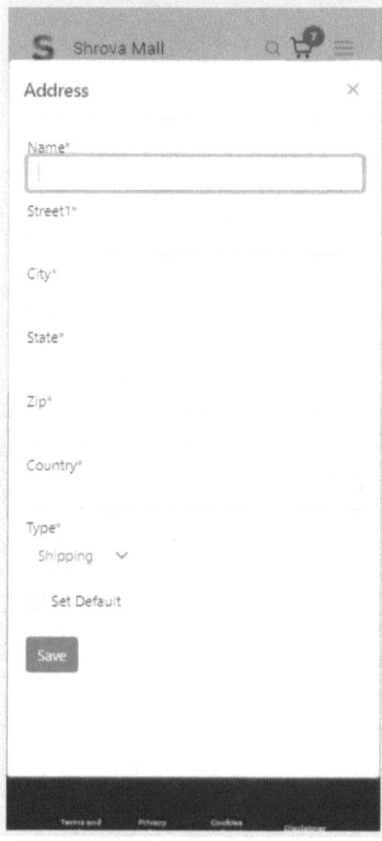

The product details page

$160

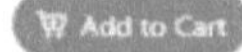

KUCCU Stand Food Mixer, 6.5 Qt 660W

Description

6.5 QUART HIGH CAPACITY - 660W high performance motor, Big stainless steel mixing bowl offers enough capacity. Each Kuccu kitchen stand mixer comes with a dough hook, flat beater, wire whip, and pouring shield avoiding mess kneading process. You can enjoy the fun of making cakes, bread, cookies, pastry, muffins and waffle.

About   Contact

Subscribe Now

of making cakes, bread, cookies, pastry, muffins and waffle.

About   Contact

Subscribe Now

Get notified upon new content!

Your email

Subscribe

Terms and Conditions   Privacy Policy   Cookies Policy   Disclaimer

Copyright Notice   DMCA Policy   Refund Policy   Terms of Sale

S

The category page

The search/filter page

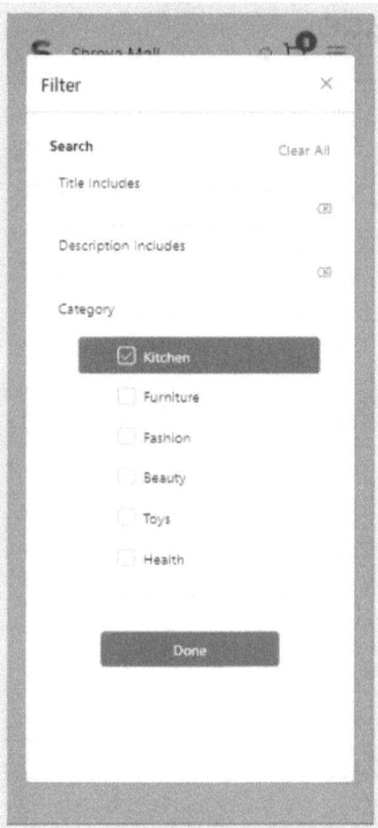
Shreya Mall
Filter
Search
Clear All
Title Includes
Description Includes
Category
Kitchen
Furniture
Fashion
Beauty
Toys
Health
Done

The cart page

 Nuwave Bravo
Air Fryer Toaster
Smart Oven

$170

Remove   -   1   →

Continue to Shipping

Subtotal(7 items) $1205

Taxes   Calculated at checkout

Estimated Total $1205

The shipping page

Rates

FASTEST

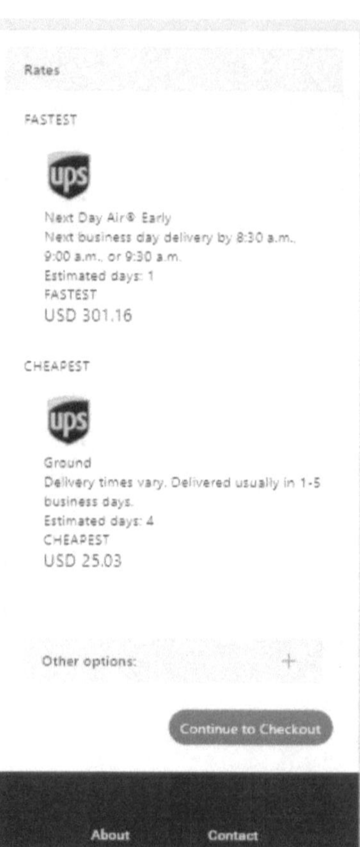

Next Day Air® Early
Next business day delivery by 8:30 a.m.,
9:00 a.m., or 9:30 a.m.
Estimated days: 1
FASTEST
USD 301.16

CHEAPEST

Ground
Delivery times vary. Delivered usually in 1-5
business days.
Estimated days: 4
CHEAPEST
USD 25.03

Other options: +

Continue to Checkout

About   Contact

The summary page

 Nuwave Bravo Air Fryer
Toaster Smart Oven

1    $170 $170

Subtotal(7 items) $1205

Shipping $301.16

Estimated Total $1506.16

Continue to Payment

About   Contact

Subscribe Now

Get notified upon new content!

Your email

Subscribe

The payment page

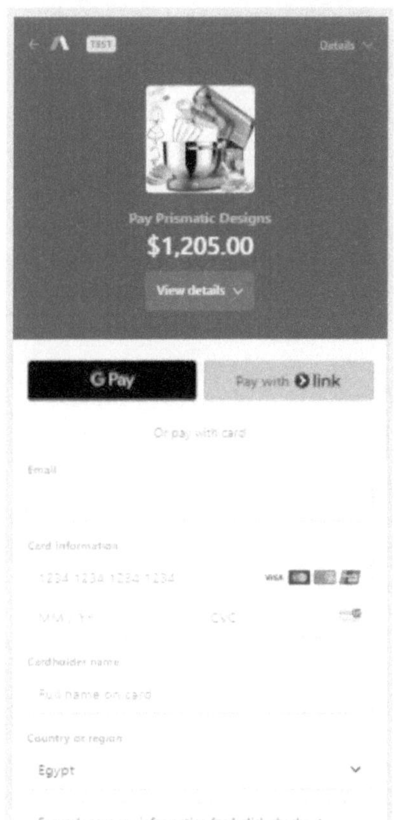

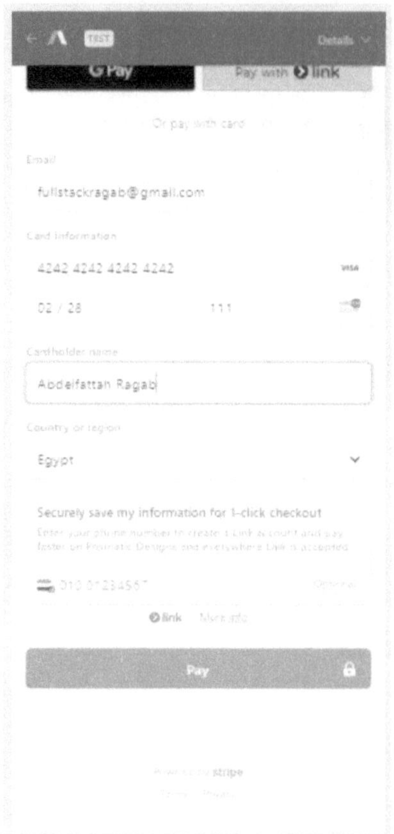

During development, we use a test key from Stripe, which we replace with the live key as soon as we are finished. This way you can test the full cycle with payments without paying real money until you go live. To go live, you simply use the live key instead of the test key.

The success page

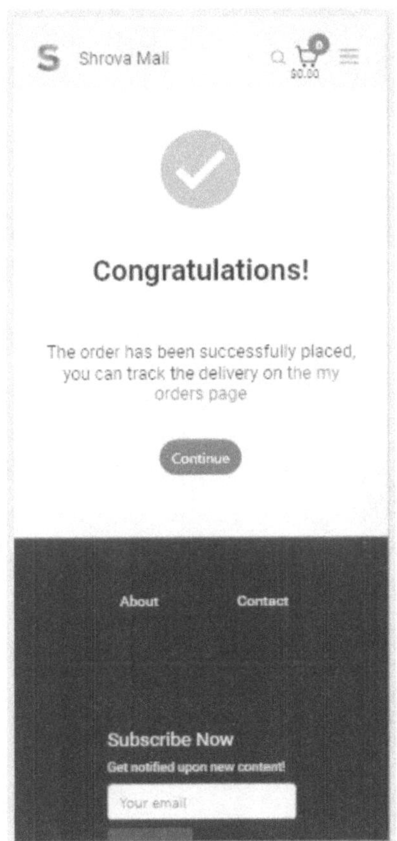

The cancel page

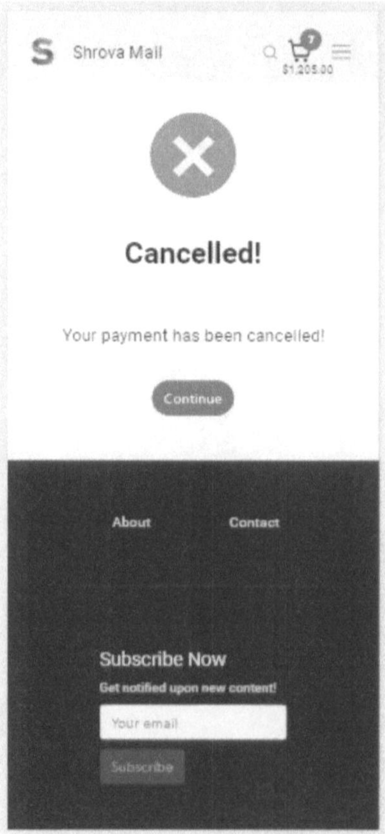

The my orders page

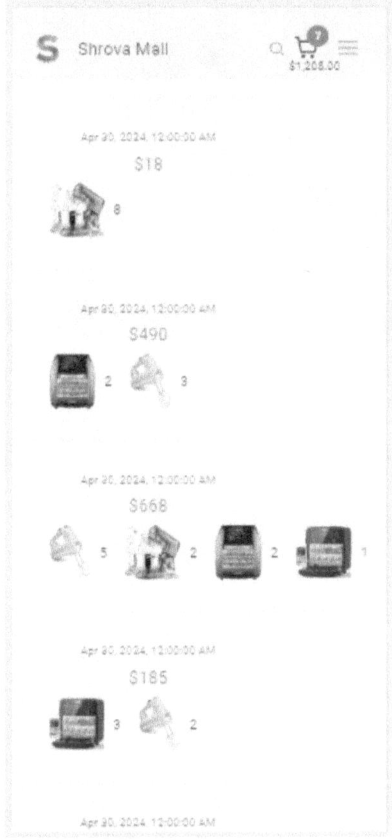

The application is fully responsive and also works on the desktop.

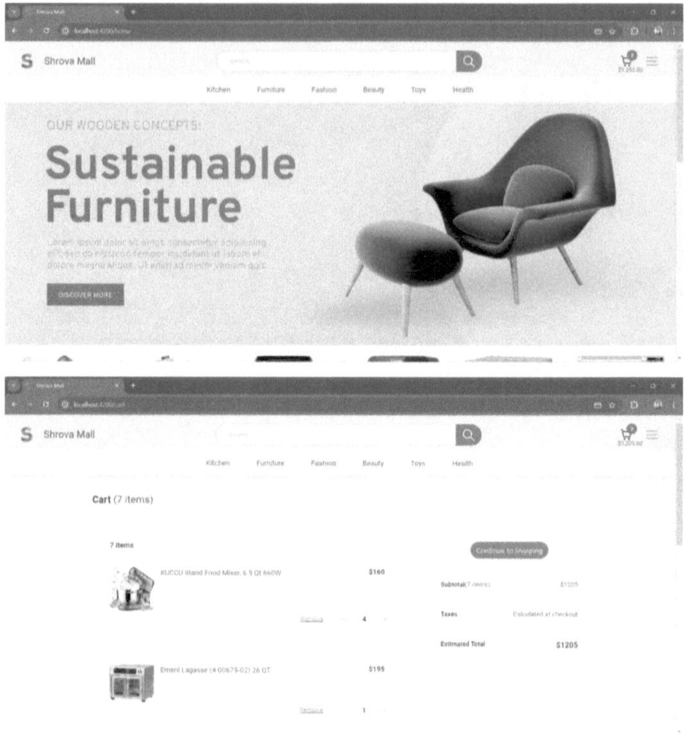

User scenarios

Almost all of us are familiar with online shopping and we place many online orders from time to time.
We are familiar with the process and it is the same for almost all online stores.
Usually you visit the store's website and search for the product, add it to your shopping cart, enter the shipping details and pay online.

You can view your order history and track the delivery of your shipment.
Since you are the owner of the store this time, I have added more pages to manage products and store details.
Our store will have all the features you find in all the big stores in the world.
You will need to add more promotional components to your store to make it more attractive to customers, but I'll leave that up to you. I will mainly focus on the core features like authentication, product management, shipping, payments and so on.
The application is fully optimized for mobile devices and desktops.

To make it even clearer, I'll explain how we can use the application for different scenarios.

Admin

A typical use case for the admin includes the following steps

Register new user

The first thing the user encounters when visiting the website is the homepage.
At the top right is the "Sign Up" button, which takes the user to the registration page.

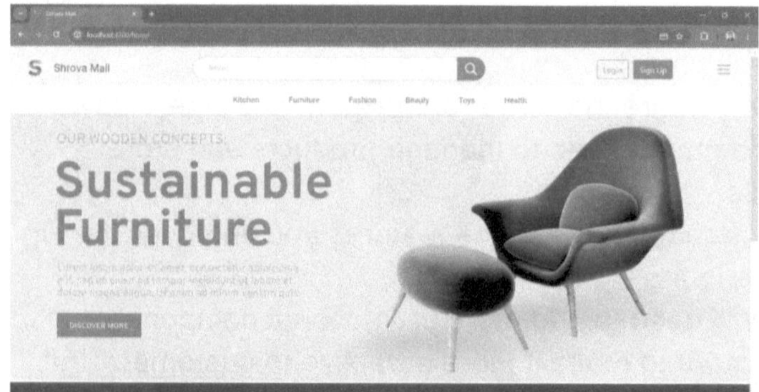

By filling in the required data and clicking on "Sign Up", the user has now created a new user in the system.

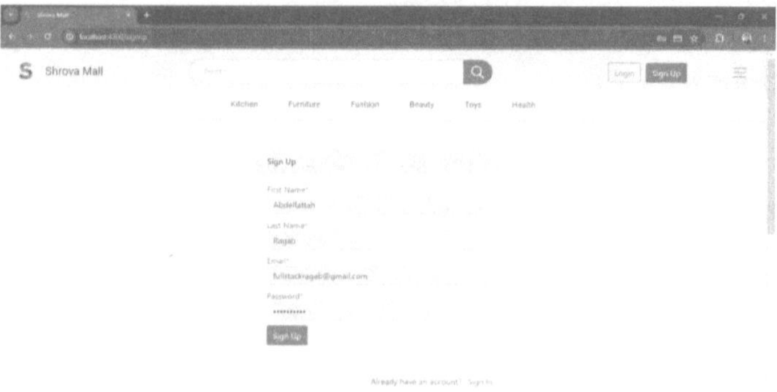

Login

New users are automatically logged in, and the refresh token remains active for a period of 7 days, after which it expires and prompts the user to log in again. Would it be better to use a shorter period for security reasons?
Sure. The 7 days is the period of the refresh token, not the access token. The lifetime of the access token is 5 minutes, which means that a new access token is

issued every five minutes based on the 7-day refresh token. Requests are automatically processed with new tokens and repeated without user intervention to ensure a seamless user experience with best-in-class security metrics.

After successful login, the shopping cart icon is displayed in the top right corner. You may want to change this behavior and allow guests to add products to the cart and delay logging in until they proceed to checkout. I found this unnecessary as they can't complete orders without logging in, so I started asking them to register only when they want to buy products. You can agree to this or not.

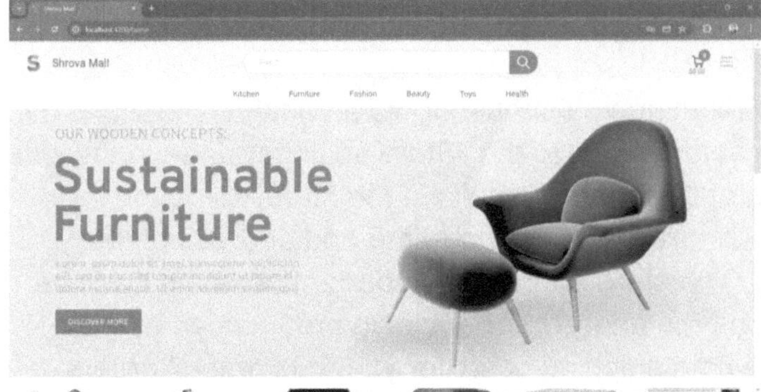

To make a user an admin, you must set the isAdmin flag to true in the database. There is no option in the application to make a user an admin.

After you have set it as admin in the database, you must log out of the application and log in again so that the application is loaded as admin.

Store settings

The first thing you should do as an admin is to make the store settings. Go to the "Store settings" page in the side menu and enter the details of the store.
You will need to enter the name and address of the store. The store address is important because it will be used as the address for shipping products and calculating shipping costs for your customers' orders.

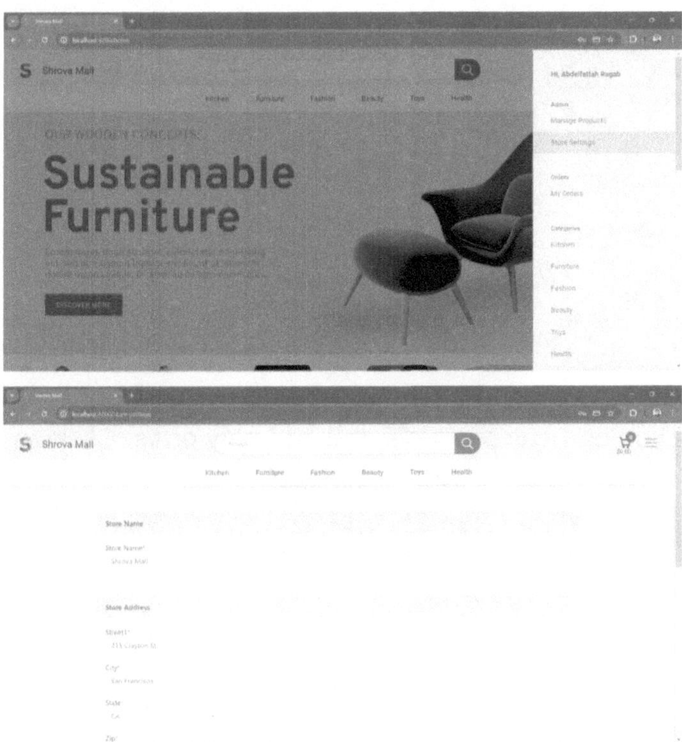

Manage products

Now let's add some products to our new store. Go to the "Manage products" page via the side menu.

Here you can edit products and add new ones. Click on the "+Add" button to add new products.

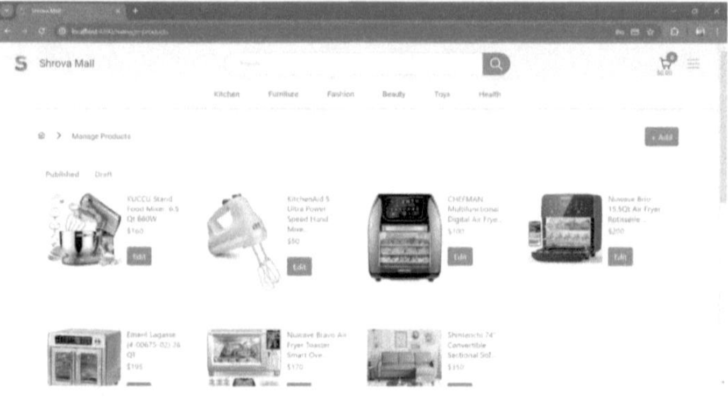

Add new product

Let's add a new product

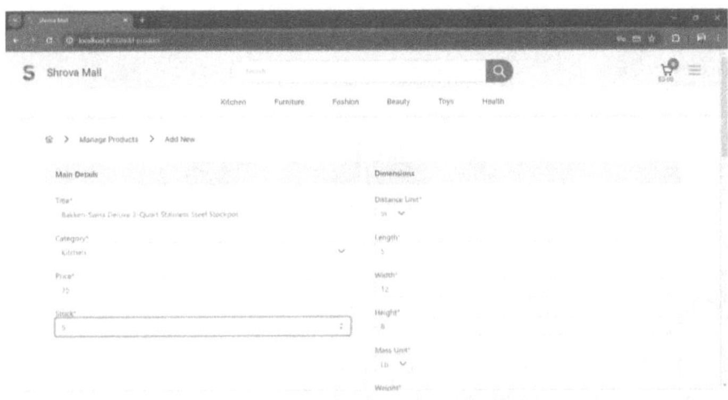

Shrova Mall
Kitchen   Furniture   Fashion   Beauty   Toys   Health
Manage Products > Add New
Main Details
Title*
Bakken-Swiss Deluxe 3-Quart Stainless Steel Stockpot
Category*
Kitchen
Price*
35
Stock*
5
Dimensions
Distance Unit*
in
Length*
5
Width*
12
Height*
8
Mass Unit*
lb
Weight*

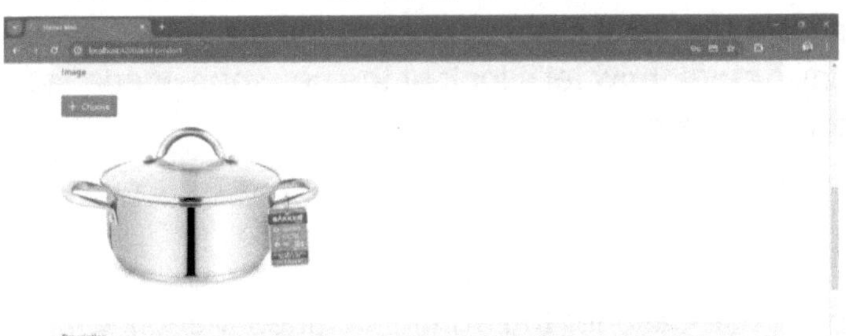

Image
+ Choose
Description
B I U G   Normal   Normal   A   Sans Serif
This stainless steel stockpot is carefully designed for every cooktop in any kitchen - create delicious dishes on gas, induction, or halogen stovetops. Think of all the dishes you could put together with our big steel pot: from stews and soups to rice dishes and turkey gravy.

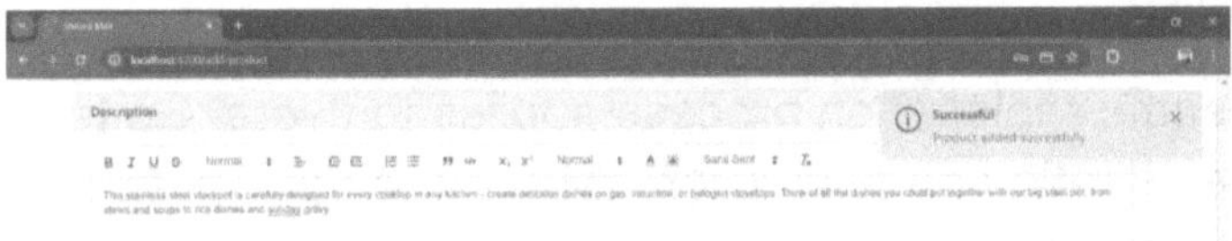

Description
B I U G   Normal   Normal   A   Sans Serif
This stainless steel stockpot is carefully designed for every cooktop in any kitchen - create delicious dishes on gas, induction, or halogen stovetops. Think of all the dishes you could put together with our big steel pot: from stews and soups to rice dishes and turkey gravy.
Successful
Product added successfully
Save   Published

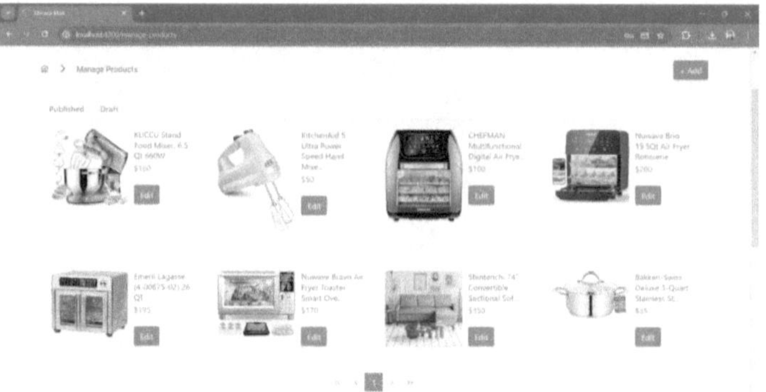

These are the most common scenarios for administrators, now let's look at the common scenarios for normal users.

User

A typical use case for the admin includes the following steps

Register new user

The same registration process applies to users. Go to the registration page by clicking on the "Sign Up" button at the top right.

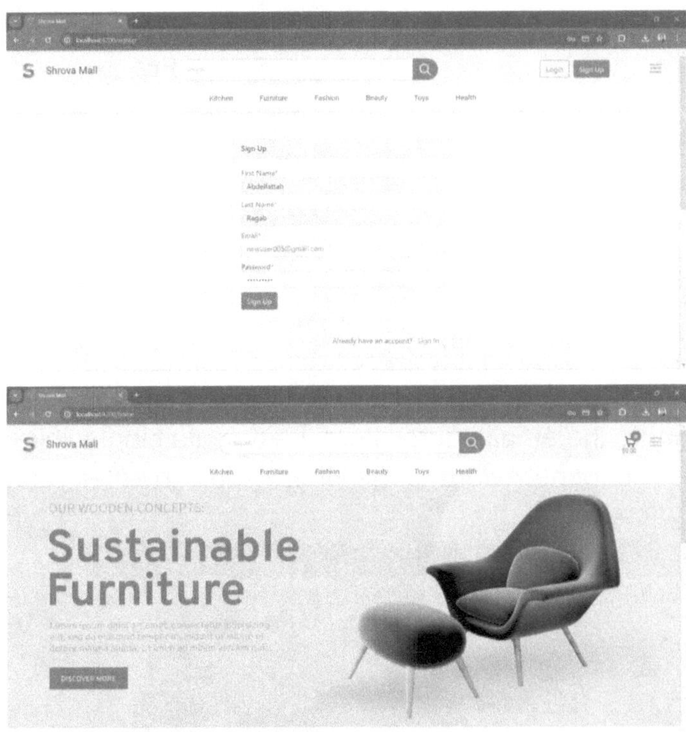

Forgot password

Users can change their password at any time by selecting "Forgot password" on the login page.
If you click on the "Forgot password" button, you will be redirected to a page where you can enter your email address.

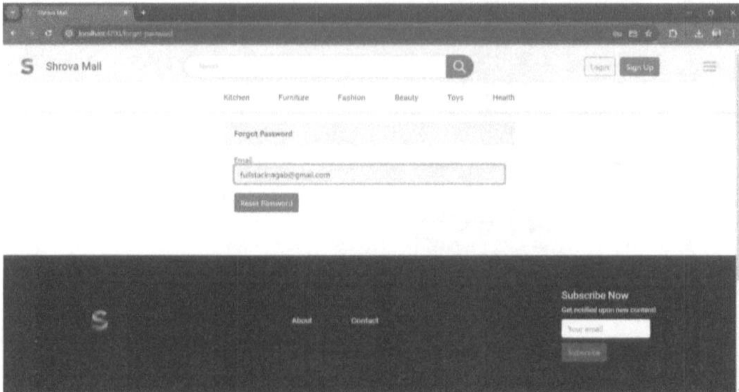

If you click on the "Reset password" button, an email will be sent to the email address provided containing a link to the "Reset password" page where you can enter your new password.

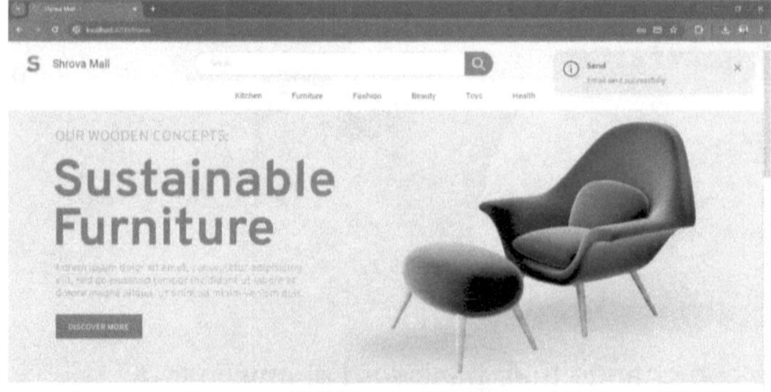

It may end up in the spam folder, so check that too. The email looks like this and the "Reset password" link has a token embedded and here is the full link in the email

https://shrovamall.com/reset-password?token=a90
c4b8800615137.badf178d385e12d32e41dd1760ca964a0
9480c0c27170cb3b2f25ac2200209d6&email=fullstack
ragab@gmail.com

When you submit a new password, a token is appended
to the request, the same token that was sent to the
email. It is compared to the token that was stored in the
user table in the database when he started the
password reset process. It must match within the
specified time period of one hour, otherwise it will be
rejected.

Fill your profile

You can change your first name and surname on your
profile page.
The other important part of the profile page is the
Addresses tab, where you can enter your billing and
shipping address.

You can add as many addresses as you like and specify which one should be used by default for shipping and invoicing.
The default shipping address is automatically used to fill in the shipping details when purchasing new products.

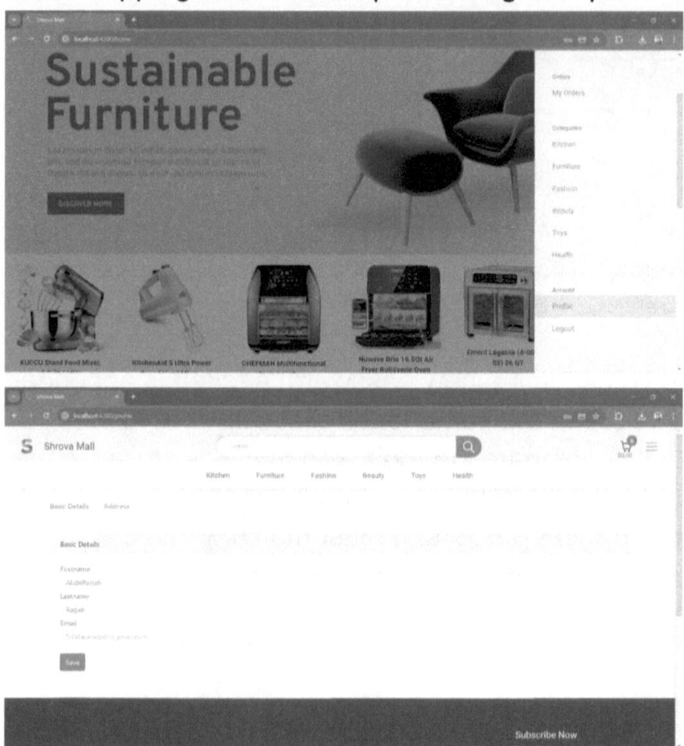

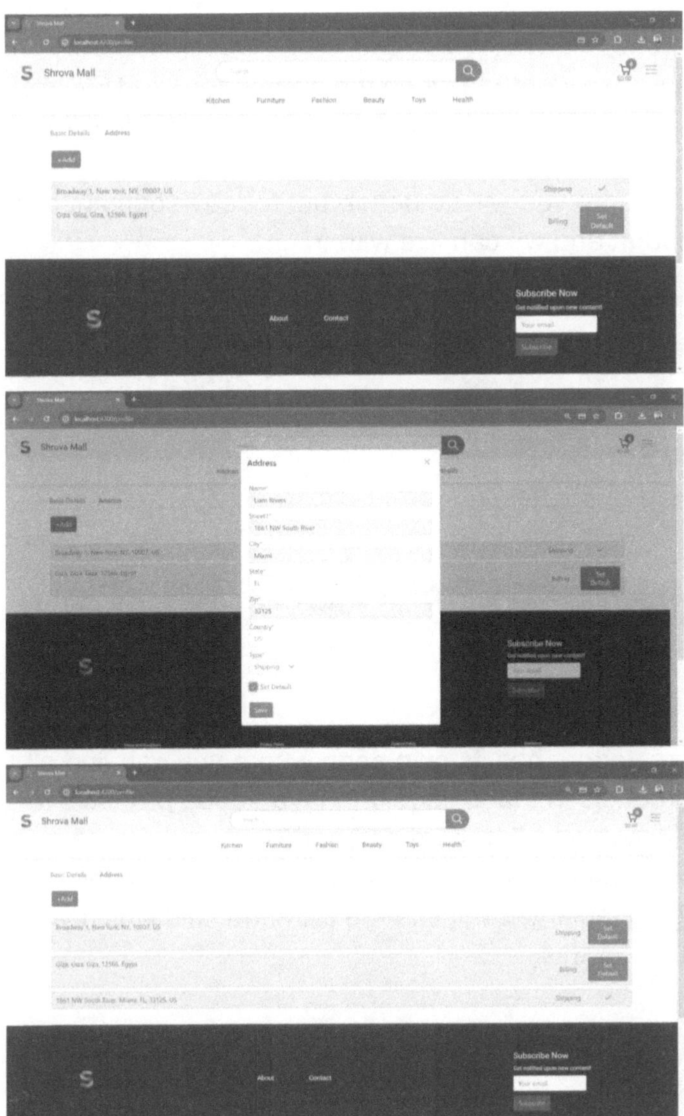

Now, it is time for shopping.

Products on the homepage

All stores have products on the homepage, and we are
no exception, so I have added some products to the
homepage for users to buy.
In your store you will do better, but for development this
is enough and we can live with it.

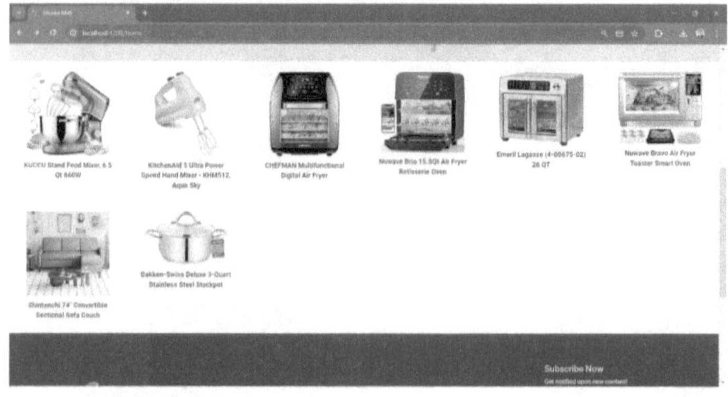

Products on the category page

Each category has its own page where you can find all
the products in that category. I have added products to
the Kitchen and Furniture categories.
The categories can also have subcategories. In the
category table you will find the parentId field which you
can use for this.

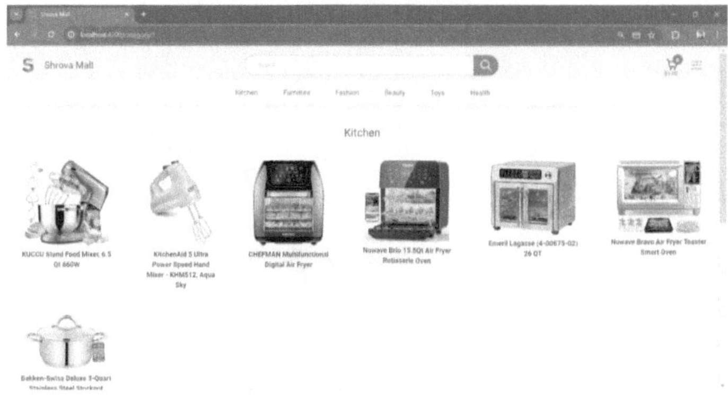

Search for products

You can search for products by tapping on the main search bar, which will then take you to the search and filter page.

On the search page, you can filter products by title, description or category.

You can add further functions to this page, e.g. sorting. To do this, you just need to add another parameter in the backend api request and execute the corresponding function in the frontend.

As these details vary from store to store, I have contented myself with the basic functions. However, the page can be extended with new functions.

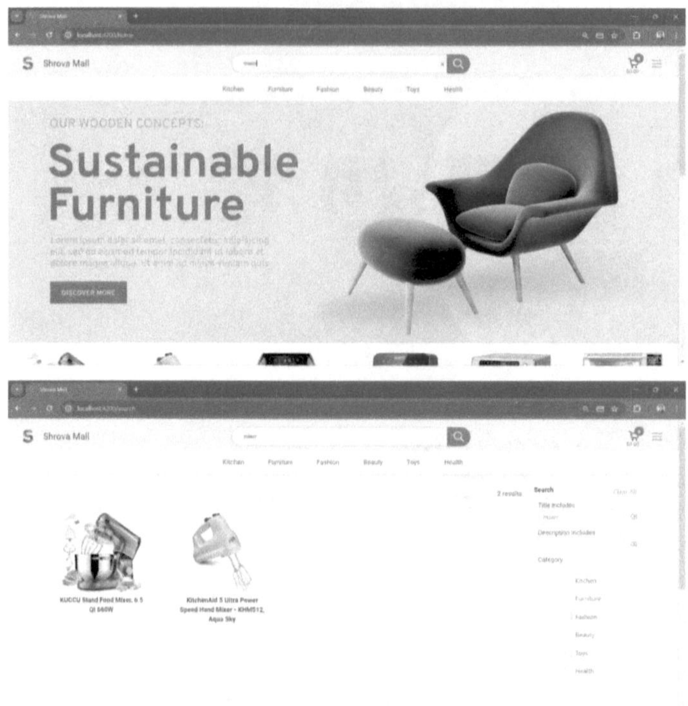
Shrova Mall
Kitchen   Furniture   Fashion   Beauty   Toys   Health
OUR WOODEN CONCEPTS:
Sustainable
Furniture
DISCOVER MORE

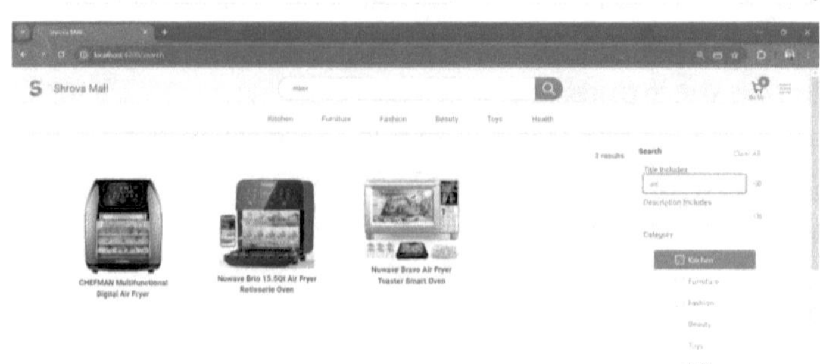
Shrova Mall
mixer
Kitchen   Furniture   Fashion   Beauty   Toys   Health
2 results
Search   Clear All
Title Includes
mixer
Description Includes
Category
Kitchen
Furniture
Fashion
Beauty
Toys
Health
KUCCU Stand Food Mixer, 6 5
Qt 660W
KitchenAid 5 Ultra Power
Speed Hand Mixer - KHM512,
Aqua Sky

Shrova Mall
mixer
Kitchen   Furniture   Fashion   Beauty   Toys   Health
3 results
Search   Clear All
Title Includes
air
Description Includes
Category
Kitchen
Furniture
Fashion
Beauty
Toys
Health
CHEFMAN Multifunctional
Digital Air Fryer
Nuwave Brio 15.5Qt Air Fryer
Rotisserie Oven
Nuwave Bravo Air Fryer
Toaster Smart Oven

Add products to shopping cart

Anywhere in the system, on the home page, the category page or the search and filter page. You can click on the product you want to buy and you will be redirected to the product detail page.

You'll have a better detail page for your store, but for this project, I'll go with this.

Click on the "Add to shopping cart" button to add the product to your shopping cart.

Each click on the "Add to cart" button adds something to the cart.
You can check and change the quantity of products on the shopping cart page.

Shopping cart

In the shopping cart you can change the quantities of the products or remove them from the shopping cart.

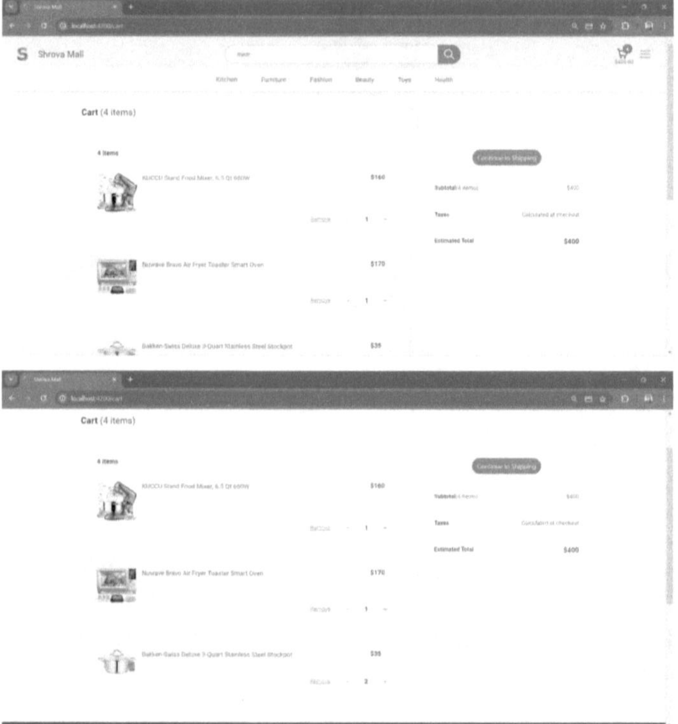

When you are ready, go to the next step. Click on "Continue to Shipping".

Select shipping method

First you have to enter the delivery address. If you have set the default delivery address, it will be loaded automatically.

After you have entered the delivery address, a list of delivery methods will be displayed from which you can select one.

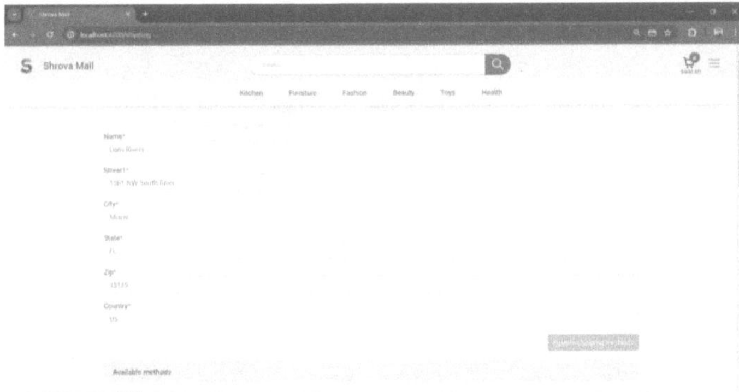

Whenever you change the delivery address, you must update the shipping methods.

I have placed the three methods "Best value for money", "Fastest" and "Cheapest" at the top and all other options are hidden, but you can still access them if you want to choose one of them.

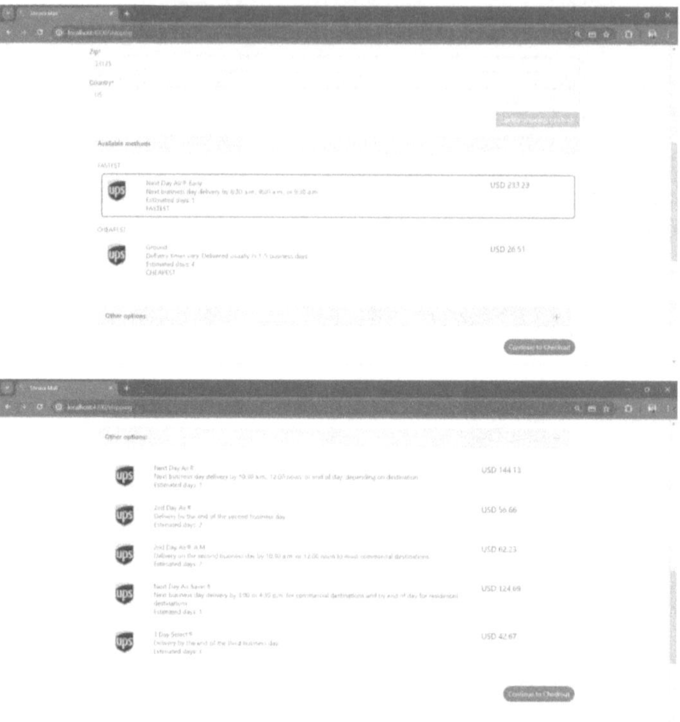

For shipping, I use the service provider Shippo, which works with many providers, not just UPS. However, these details are determined at runtime based on the source and destination addresses and many other variables.

You can visit your Shippo account to manage all these details.

Once you have selected the shipping method, you can proceed to the next step by clicking on the "Proceed to checkout" button.

The order summary

The last step is the order summary, where you can check everything before you make the payment. These pages should be better designed, but I'll leave that up to you.

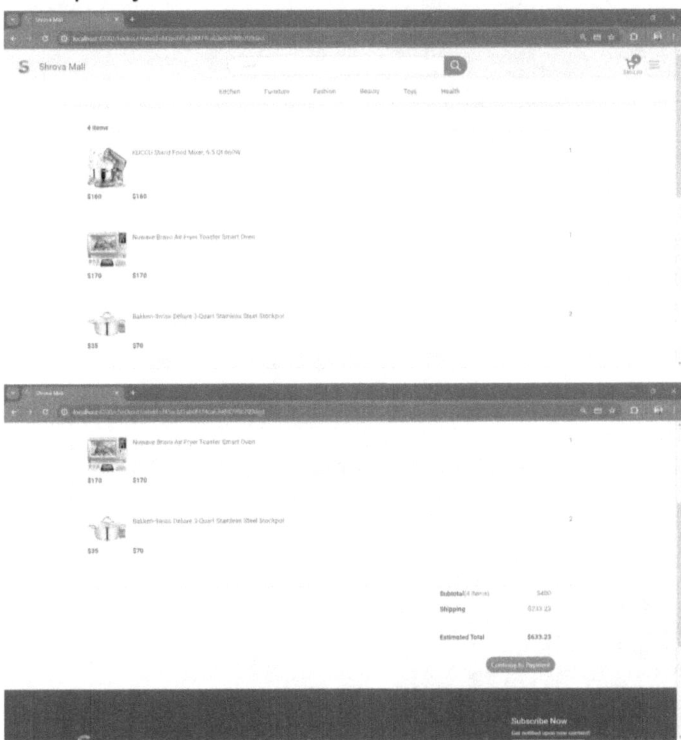

When you have finished checking your order, you can proceed to the last step, the payment step. Click on "Continue to Payment".

Payment

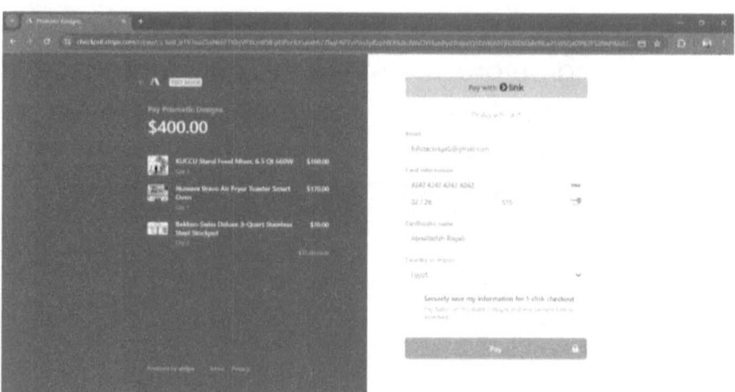

We are in test mode, in which we can use the test card number 4242. No real payment is made, but programmatically all processes are executed.
When we go live, the only change will be that we use a live key instead of the test key. Everything else will remain the same.

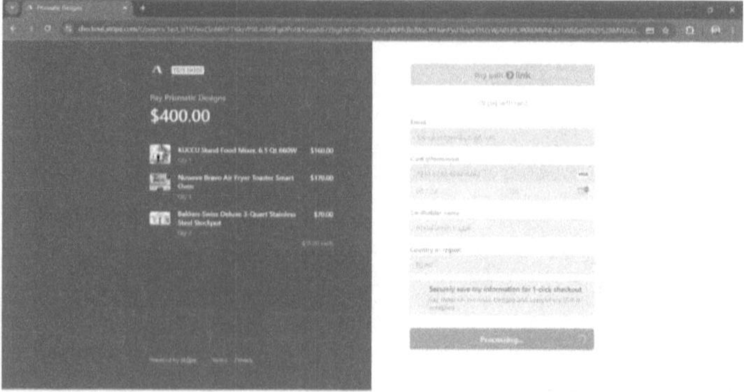

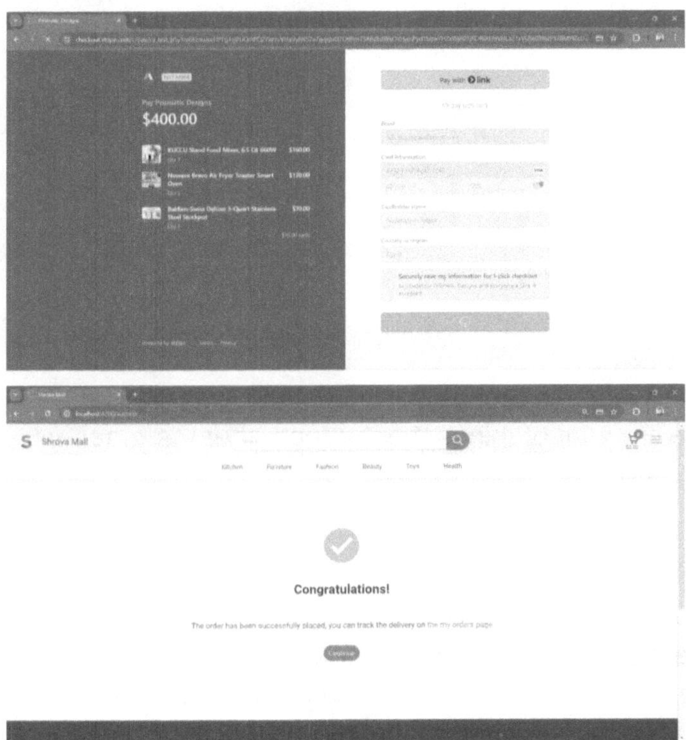

Success or cancel

If the user has successfully completed the order, he will be redirected to the success page; if he has canceled the payment, he will be redirected to the cancelation page.

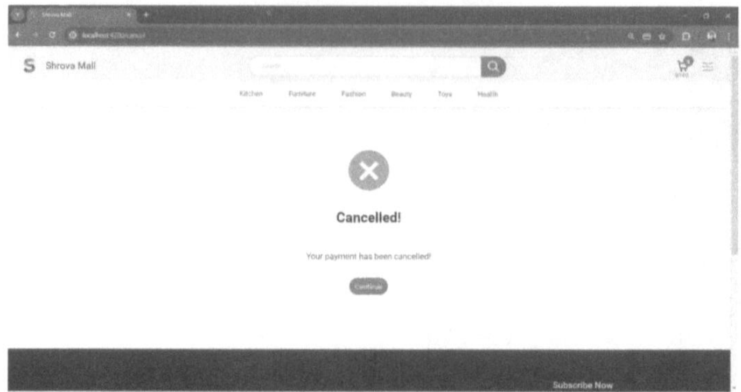

That's what the user gets, but on the backend side, there are a lot of things that happen after the order is completed.

The payment process

Let me explain the process from the beginning to understand what exactly happens.
When the user clicks on the "Add to cart" button, the "Add product" method of the cart service is invoked, which adds the product to the product list or increments it by one if it already exists.

After the cart has been updated, the saveCart method is called to save the cart in the database. It first converts the cart object into a string and sends it to the backend server, which saves it in the database under the current user ID.

When the application is loaded for the first time or when you refresh the page, loadCart from the backend converts the string into a cart object and sets it as the current cart.

Let's continue with the explanation of the order process. Now we are on the shopping cart page. You can change the quantities or remove products from the cart.
When you are finished with the products in the shopping cart, you can move on to the next step: shipping.

On the shipping page, enter the name and delivery address and select the shipping method. The prices are calculated based on the delivery address. If you change the address details, you will have to recalculate the shipping costs. Select a rate and go to the next step.

Go to the order summary page. The Order Summary page summarizes all order details, the items in the shopping cart and the selected shipping rate and saves everything in a new record in the Order Summary table in the database and returns its ID.

The order summary ID is the only thing you will need later, as it contains all the details of the order.

After you have checked the summary, you can click on the "Proceed to payment" button and start the payment process. A new checkout session will be created on Stripe and the ID will be returned to the frontend application, which will then redirect you to the payment page on Stripe.

So far nothing has happened on the server side, i.e. if the user has not completed the payment and presses the back button or closes the application, nothing happens, we have only saved a record in the order overview table.

When the user starts the payment session on Stripe by providing valid payment details, Stripe triggers the webhook with the checkout.session.completed event and sends him the payment intent details.
I have created a table in the database with the same name "payment Intent" to store the payment intent details of the orders.
So when I receive the payment intent data from Stripe, I store it in this table with the userId and orderSummaryId.
Now I wait for the event "payment_intent.succeeded", which means that the payment has been successfully completed and the money has been successfully transferred to your Stripe account. This allows me to say that the order has been successfully completed and I can deliver the product to the customer.
In the event "payment_intent.succeeded" I do many things. I create a new order object, which I will soon save in the database. I purchase the shipping label from shippo for the selected rate and add the labelUrl with all the tracking information to the order object. I also add the userId, the summaryId, the transObjId, the items in the order with their quantities, the total amount, the order date and the paymentintentId. Some of these details are not important to the customer, but I store

them for reference in case there are any issues with payment or shipping so you have the IDs for customer support.

After I add all these details to the order object, I save it to the database. I also delete all the temporary records of the payment intentions and the shopping cart.

In the frontend, Stripe redirects to the success page if the payment was successful. On the success page, I delete the shopping cart and allow the user to place a new order.

The user can view the order history on the My Orders page. All orders are provided with tracking information so that the user can track the shipment on the provider's website.

How to create this application

Many levels of technology are involved in the development of this application. Front-end technologies, back-end technologies and database technologies.

The front-end level, which refers to the development of applications that work on the end device such as the cell phone or desktop. These applications run in the browser and are called front-end applications. Mostly we use JavaScript and there are many frameworks for front-end application development such as Angular, React and Vue.

Front-end applications are designed exclusively for end users and are responsible for all user interactions, such as receiving input and returning results to users.

Workflows, business decisions and calculations are managed by another group of applications, the backend applications, which are hosted online and not on the user's computer.

There are many technologies used to develop backend applications, e.g. .NET, Java, NodeJS, PHP and many more.

The third layer is the database layer, which is hosted on database servers. This layer is only responsible for storing data and is managed by the backend application, which connects to the database to store and retrieve application data.

To develop a software application, you use programming languages and write code that is compiled into a working application.

To write the code, we use special editors. The most common of these is Visual Studio Code.

To maintain the codebase, we use a technology called Git. Git is a well-known technology that is responsible for managing all code-related tasks.

After we have completed the development, we need to deploy our application. We need to put it online so that users can use it.

Front-end applications are deployed on static hosting. After you have deployed the application, you need to connect it to a custom domain like https://shrovamall.com

The backend is deployed on a web service hosting and is given a URL that you will use as the base URL for the API endpoints.

There are also service providers for hosting the database who will provide you with the connection details such as the hosting name etc. after deployment. For other services like shipping and payment, each service provider will give you an apiKey that you need to attach to each request to get the appropriate response. Shippo, Stripe and Firebase will give you apiKeys. Development is a continuous process. After you put your code online, you may need to make changes and deploy it again.

This process is automatically managed by Git.

When you push the changed code from your local machine online to the GitHub server, a webhook is triggered, which is intercepted by Render.com to start rebuilding and redeploying your application.

Used technologies

Frontend

Angular

We use the latest Angular version at the time of publication of the book, namely Angular 18

Packages used are:
- `@stripe/stripe-js`
- `ngx-quill`
- `primeicons`

- primeng

Backend

NestJs

We use the latest NestJS version at the time of publication of the book, namely NestJS 10

Packages used are:
- `@nestjs/jwt`
- `@nestjs/mapped-types`
- `@nestjs/passport`
- `@nestjs/platform-express`
- `@nestjs/typeorm`
- `class-transformer`
- `class-validator`
- `firebase`
- `nodemailer`
- `passport`
- `passport-jwt`
- `passport-local`
- `pg`
- `shippo`
- `stripe`
- `typeorm`

Database

PostgreSQL

We use the latest PostgreSQL version at the time of publication of the book, namely PostgreSQL 16, hosted on Render.com

Payments

Stripe

We use the latest Stripe version at the time of publication of the book, namely Stripe 2024-04-10

Shipping

Shippo

We use the latest Shippo version at the time of publication of the book, namely Shippo Version 2018-02-08 released on Apr 29 2024

Codebase Management

Git

We use the latest Git version at the time of publication of the book, namely Git 2.45.0

Deployment

Render.com

We use the latest Render.com version at the time of publication of the book.

Development steps

You need accounts with GitHub, Firebase, Gmail, Render.com, Stripe and Shippo.

Let me first explain why you need each of these accounts.

GitHub
You need GitHub to take care of your source code.

Firebase
We will store the product images in Firebase

Gmail
We will use Gmail to send password reset emails to users

Render.com
Render.com will be the hosting service provider where we will deploy all our applications and the database.

Stripe

You will receive money to your Stripe account.

Shippo
Shippo takes care of shipping the products to the customers

Here's what you need to do to create your online store

Log in to your Render.com account and create a new PostgreSQL database with the Starter Plan. The free plan is not intended for businesses and has many limitations. The data will be deleted after 90 days.

Log in to your GitHub account and create two private repositories for your projects, one for the frontend project and one for the backend.

Create two projects on your local computer: an Angular project for the frontend and a NestJS project for the backend.

Connect each project to the corresponding GitHub repository.

Now go to Render.com and create two new services, a static service for the frontend and a web service for the backend.
The static service is free, but you need to pay for the backend service. You can opt for the Starter plan.

Render creates services based on GitHub repositories. This means that you need to tell Render the GitHub repository of the service and Render will retrieve the code from GitHub, build it and deploy it online.

Once all the services are set up, the final step is to connect your website to your own domain. You buy your domain, e.g. https://shrovamall.com, and connect it to your frontend service.
You can perform this step at any time once you have created the frontend service on Render.com

Now your store is ready to receive new customers online.

Well done!

Now we have completed the foundation and can start creating the database.

Create the database

As you already know from the start book, we will host everything on Render.com.
Log in to your Render account and create a new PostgreSQL database.

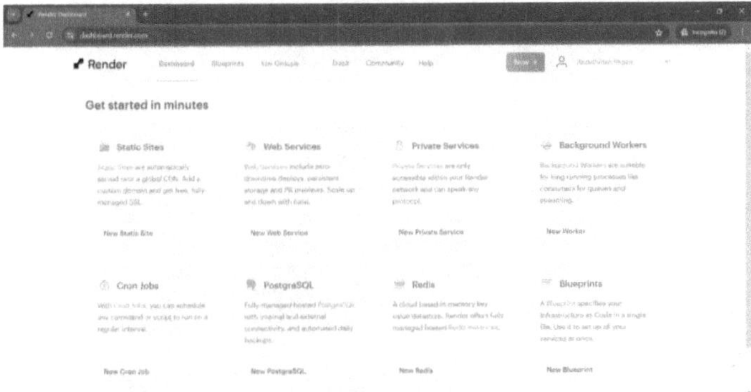

Fill in the database details and choose the "starter" plan. The "free" plan is not suitable for real business projects as it has many limitations and the data is deleted every 90 days.

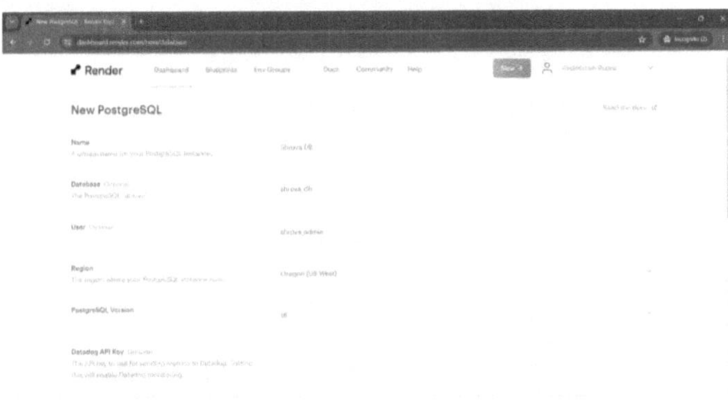

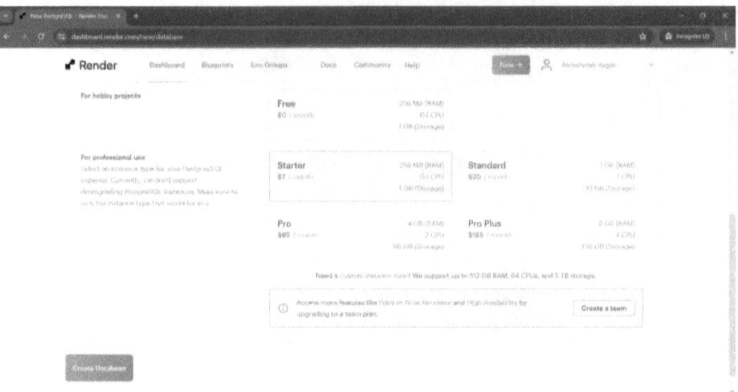

Here are the details you need to provide to create the database
database
Name: **Shrova DB**
Database: **shrova_db**
User: **shrova_admin**

Click on "Create Database"

Wait a few minutes until your database is ready.

pgAdmin

In the meantime, download pgAdmin and install it on your computer as we will use it to edit the database. Open the pgAdmin application and connect to the database.

To connect to the database, right-click on the Server entry in the Object Explorer on the left-hand side and register a new server.

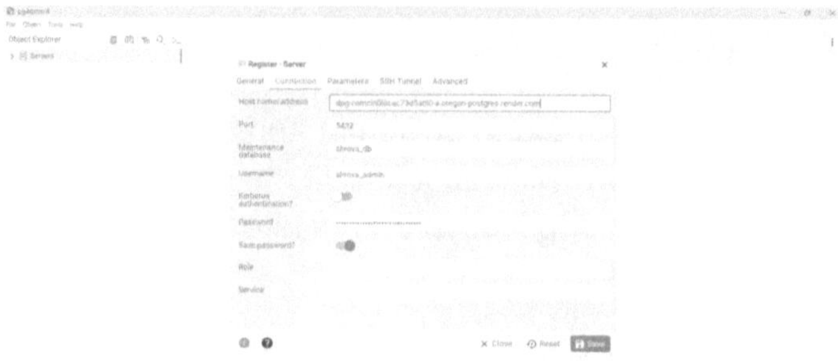

Fill in the details and connect to the server.
Host name/address:

dpg-comcln0l6cac73d5adi0-a.oregon-postgres.render.com

Port: **5432**
Maintenance database: **shrova_db**
Username: **shrova_admin**
Password: ***************

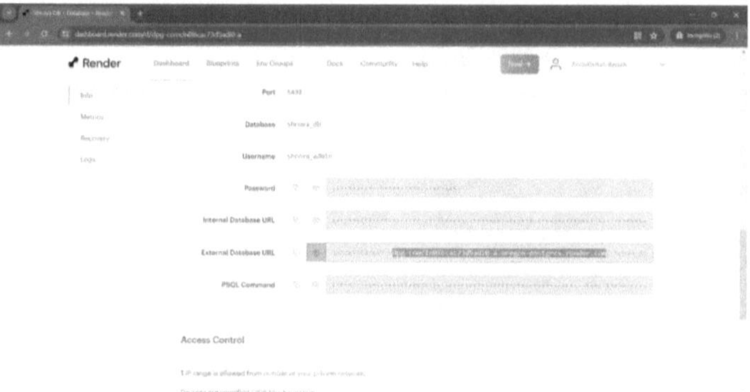

You should enter the long form of the host name that you find at the end of the external URL because you are connecting from outside the render network.

If you are connecting from inside the render network, you can use the short hostname and connect without SSL.

Now you are connected to the database, so let's create the tables.

All tables have the id column as primary key with auto-increment. For this to work, they need sequences, so let's create the sequences first.

I will create sequences for the id column of each table.

At the beginning I want to explain to you which tables we need in our application and here is a list of all the tables we will create.

Database tables

- address
- cart
- category
- default_address
- newsletter
- order
- order_summary
- payment_intent
- product
- store_settings
- user

address

Each user can have multiple addresses for shipping and billing. We save them all with the userId in the address table.

Here are the columns of the address table:

- id
- userId
- street1
- city
- state
- zip
- country
- type
- name

The "type" column has one of the two values 1 for billing and 2 for shipping.

cart

After each interaction with the shopping cart, we save the status of the shopping cart in the database. When the user closes the application to come back later or continue on another device, he/she will find the same shopping cart as when he/she left it.
If you add items, change the quantity or delete items, the shopping cart object is updated in the database.
When the user completes his/her order, we delete all shopping cart records in the database that relate to the current user.
Here are the columns of the cart table:
- id
- userId
- cart

Before we send the cart object to the backend to store it in the database, we convert it into a string.
When we load it later, we convert it back into an object and load it in the frontend application.

category

Sores classifies products into categories such as kitchen, furniture and so on.

The details of the categories are stored in the category table. The categories can be arranged hierarchically using the parentId field to create subcategories.
Here are the columns of the category table:
- id
- title
- parentId
- order

You can use the "order" field to determine the order of the categories on the page

default_address

If you have many addresses, you can decide which one is the default address. We store this information as one data record for each address type in the default_address table. So each user can have a maximum of two records, one for the default billing address and one for the default delivery address.
Here are the columns of the default_address table:
- id
- userId
- addressId
- addressType

newsletter

Anyone can sign up for the store's newsletter and we save their emails in the newsletter table. The active flag is here to set it to false when a user unsubscribes from the mailing list, or you can delete the record from the table if you wish.
Here are the columns of the newsletter table:
- id
- email
- active

order

The order table contains all the details of the user's successfully completed orders.
Here are the columns of the order table:
- id
- userId
- orderDate
- items
- total
- labelUrl
- trackingNumber
- trackingUrl
- transObjId
- paymentIntentId
- summaryId

order_summary

Once the user has reviewed the order summary and clicked the "Continue to payment" button, we save the order summary in the database. We will use this record later to create the order object after the user has completed the payment.
Here are the columns of the order_summary table:
- id
- userId
- orderDate
- items
- total
- rateId

payment_intent

When the user starts the payment process, Stripe creates a checkout session and sends us the payment Intent object.
We store the payment intent details in the database and wait until we receive the payment_intent.succeeded event from Stripe, which means that the money is now in your account and you can confidently complete the order.
Here are the columns of the payment_intent table:
- id
- paymentIntentId
- userId
- summaryId

product

The product table stores product details such as title, price, width, weight, height and so on.
Here are the columns of the product table:

- id
- title
- description
- category
- imageUrl
- published
- price
- stock
- length
- width
- height
- distanceUnit
- weight
- massUnit

The "published" field is used to decide whether the product should be visible to users or not. If there are orders set for the product and you cannot delete it, you can set "published" to "false" instead and move it to draft status.

store_settings

The store_settings table stores information about the store, such as the name of the store and the address of the store.
This address is used to send products to customers.
Here are the columns of the store_settings table:

- id
- storeName
- street1
- city
- state
- zip
- country

user

The user table stores user details such as first name, last name and so on.
Here are the columns of the user table:

- id
- firstname
- lastname
- email
- password
- resetPasswordToken
- tokenCreatedAt
- isAdmin

The resetPasswordToken and the tokenCreatedAt are used when resetting the user password.

Create sequences

All tables have an id column with autoincrement. So we need to create sequences for all id columns in all tables. So let's do that.

address_id_seq

```sql
-- SEQUENCE: public.address_id_seq

-- DROP SEQUENCE IF EXISTS public.address_id_seq;

CREATE SEQUENCE IF NOT EXISTS public.address_id_seq
    INCREMENT 1
    START 1
    MINVALUE 1
    MAXVALUE 2147483647
    CACHE 1;

ALTER SEQUENCE public.address_id_seq
    OWNER TO shrova_admin;
```

Here is the script to create the sequence, that you can simply run.
You can also create the sequence with the wizard and here you can see how to do it.
Right click on "Sequences" and choose "Create" →
"Sequence"

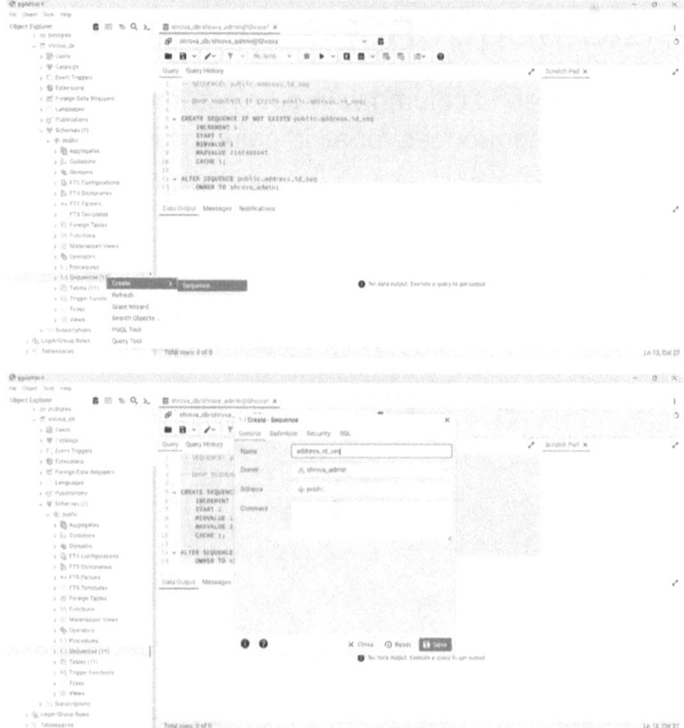

In the "General" tab set the name to "address_id_seq".

In the "Definitions" tab fill the details
Increment: **1**
Start: **1**
Minimum: **1**
Maximum: **2147483647**
Cache: **1**

Click **"Save"**

cart_id_seq

```
-- SEQUENCE: public.cart_id_seq

-- DROP SEQUENCE IF EXISTS public.cart_id_seq;

CREATE SEQUENCE IF NOT EXISTS
public.cart_id_seq
    INCREMENT 1
    START 1
    MINVALUE 1
    MAXVALUE 2147483647
    CACHE 1;

ALTER SEQUENCE public.cart_id_seq
    OWNER TO shrova_admin;
```

category_id_seq

```
-- SEQUENCE: public.category_id_seq
```

```sql
-- DROP SEQUENCE IF EXISTS
public.category_id_seq;

CREATE SEQUENCE IF NOT EXISTS
public.category_id_seq
    INCREMENT 1
    START 1
    MINVALUE 1
    MAXVALUE 2147483647
    CACHE 1;

ALTER SEQUENCE public.category_id_seq
    OWNER TO shrova_admin;
```

default_address_id_seq

```sql
-- SEQUENCE: public.default_address_id_seq

-- DROP SEQUENCE IF EXISTS
public.default_address_id_seq;

CREATE SEQUENCE IF NOT EXISTS
public.default_address_id_seq
    INCREMENT 1
    START 1
    MINVALUE 1
    MAXVALUE 2147483647
    CACHE 1;

ALTER SEQUENCE public.default_address_id_seq
    OWNER TO shrova_admin;
```

newsletter_id_seq

```
-- SEQUENCE: public.newsletter_id_seq

-- DROP SEQUENCE IF EXISTS
public.newsletter_id_seq;

CREATE SEQUENCE IF NOT EXISTS
public.newsletter_id_seq
    INCREMENT 1
    START 1
    MINVALUE 1
    MAXVALUE 2147483647
    CACHE 1;

ALTER SEQUENCE public.newsletter_id_seq
    OWNER TO shrova_admin;
```

order_id_seq

```
-- SEQUENCE: public.order_id_seq

-- DROP SEQUENCE IF EXISTS public.order_id_seq;

CREATE SEQUENCE IF NOT EXISTS
public.order_id_seq
    INCREMENT 1
    START 1
    MINVALUE 1
    MAXVALUE 2147483647
    CACHE 1;

ALTER SEQUENCE public.order_id_seq
    OWNER TO shrova_admin;
```

order_summary_id_seq

```
-- SEQUENCE: public.order_summary_id_seq

-- DROP SEQUENCE IF EXISTS
public.order_summary_id_seq;

CREATE SEQUENCE IF NOT EXISTS
public.order_summary_id_seq
    INCREMENT 1
    START 1
    MINVALUE 1
    MAXVALUE 2147483647
    CACHE 1;

ALTER SEQUENCE public.order_summary_id_seq
    OWNER TO shrova_admin;
```

payment_intent_id_seq

```
-- SEQUENCE: public.payment_intent_id_seq

-- DROP SEQUENCE IF EXISTS
public.payment_intent_id_seq;

CREATE SEQUENCE IF NOT EXISTS
public.payment_intent_id_seq
    INCREMENT 1
    START 1
    MINVALUE 1
    MAXVALUE 2147483647
    CACHE 1;

ALTER SEQUENCE public.payment_intent_id_seq
```

        OWNER TO shrova_admin;

product_id_seq

```sql
-- SEQUENCE: public.product_id_seq

-- DROP SEQUENCE IF EXISTS
public.product_id_seq;

CREATE SEQUENCE IF NOT EXISTS
public.product_id_seq
    INCREMENT 1
    START 1
    MINVALUE 1
    MAXVALUE 2147483647
    CACHE 1;

ALTER SEQUENCE public.product_id_seq
    OWNER TO shrova_admin;
```

store_settings_id_seq

```sql
-- SEQUENCE: public.store_settings_id_seq

-- DROP SEQUENCE IF EXISTS
public.store_settings_id_seq;

CREATE SEQUENCE IF NOT EXISTS
public.store_settings_id_seq
    INCREMENT 1
    START 1
    MINVALUE 1
    MAXVALUE 2147483647
```

```
    CACHE 1;

ALTER SEQUENCE public.store_settings_id_seq
    OWNER TO shrova_admin;
```

user_id_seq

```
-- SEQUENCE: public.user_id_seq

-- DROP SEQUENCE IF EXISTS public.user_id_seq;

CREATE SEQUENCE IF NOT EXISTS
public.user_id_seq
    INCREMENT 1
    START 1
    MINVALUE 1
    MAXVALUE 2147483647
    CACHE 1;

ALTER SEQUENCE public.user_id_seq
    OWNER TO shrova_admin;
```

Create tables

Now that we have the sequences ready, we can create the tables.

address

```
-- Table: public.address

-- DROP TABLE IF EXISTS public.address;
```

```sql
CREATE TABLE IF NOT EXISTS public.address
(
    id integer NOT NULL DEFAULT
nextval('address_id_seq'::regclass),
    "userId" integer,
    street1 character varying COLLATE
pg_catalog."default",
    city character varying COLLATE
pg_catalog."default",
    state character varying COLLATE
pg_catalog."default",
    zip character varying COLLATE
pg_catalog."default",
    country character varying COLLATE
pg_catalog."default",
    type integer,
    name character varying STORAGE PLAIN
COLLATE pg_catalog."default",
    CONSTRAINT address_pkey PRIMARY KEY (id)
)

TABLESPACE pg_default;

ALTER TABLE IF EXISTS public.address
    OWNER to shrova_admin;
```

You can use this script to create the table. You can also use the wizard to create the table, and here I'll show you how to do that.
Right click on "Tables" → "Create" → "Table"

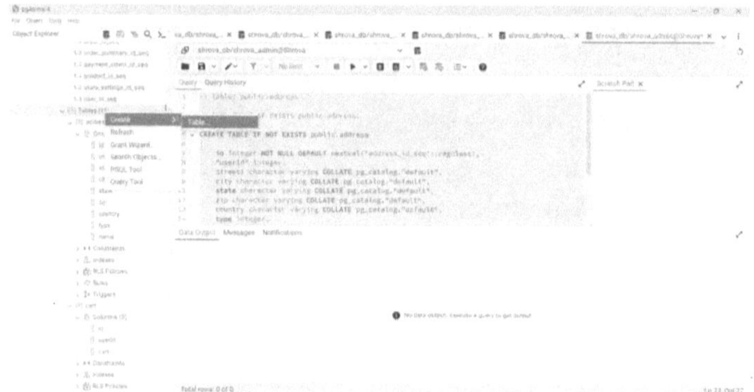

In the "General" tab, fill the table name

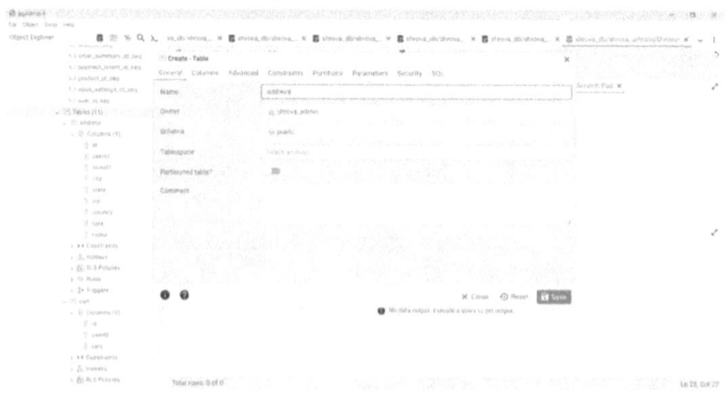

Move to the "Columns" tab and add the columns

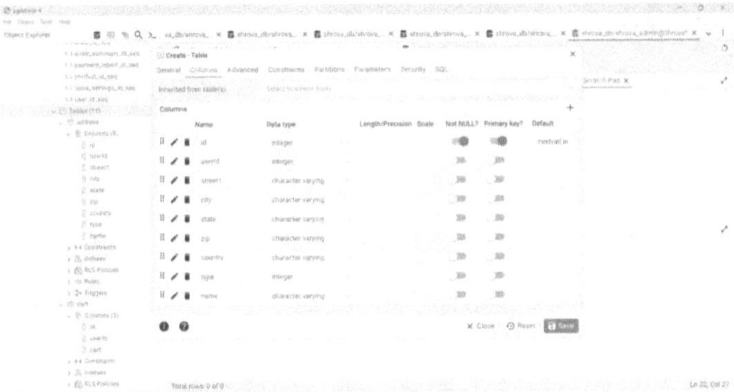

Click **"Save"**

cart

```
-- Table: public.cart

-- DROP TABLE IF EXISTS public.cart;

CREATE TABLE IF NOT EXISTS public.cart
(
    id integer NOT NULL DEFAULT
nextval('cart_id_seq'::regclass),
    "userId" integer,
    cart character varying COLLATE
pg_catalog."default",
    CONSTRAINT cart_pkey PRIMARY KEY (id)
)

TABLESPACE pg_default;

ALTER TABLE IF EXISTS public.cart
    OWNER to shrova_admin;
```

category

```
-- Table: public.category

-- DROP TABLE IF EXISTS public.category;

CREATE TABLE IF NOT EXISTS public.category
(
    id integer NOT NULL DEFAULT
nextval('category_id_seq'::regclass),
    title character varying COLLATE
pg_catalog."default",
    "parentId" integer,
    "order" integer,
    CONSTRAINT category_pkey PRIMARY KEY (id)
)

TABLESPACE pg_default;

ALTER TABLE IF EXISTS public.category
    OWNER to shrova_admin;
```

default_address

```
-- Table: public.default_address

-- DROP TABLE IF EXISTS public.default_address;

CREATE TABLE IF NOT EXISTS
public.default_address
(
    id integer NOT NULL DEFAULT
nextval('default_address_id_seq'::regclass),
    "userId" integer,
```

```sql
    "addressId" integer,
    "addressType" integer,
    CONSTRAINT default_address_pkey PRIMARY KEY
(id)
)

TABLESPACE pg_default;

ALTER TABLE IF EXISTS public.default_address
    OWNER to shrova_admin;
```

newsletter

```sql
-- Table: public.newsletter

-- DROP TABLE IF EXISTS public.newsletter;

CREATE TABLE IF NOT EXISTS public.newsletter
(
    id integer NOT NULL DEFAULT
nextval('newsletter_id_seq'::regclass),
    email character varying COLLATE
pg_catalog."default",
    active boolean NOT NULL DEFAULT true,
    CONSTRAINT newsletter_pkey PRIMARY KEY (id)
)

TABLESPACE pg_default;

ALTER TABLE IF EXISTS public.newsletter
    OWNER to shrova_admin;
```

order

```sql
-- Table: public.order

-- DROP TABLE IF EXISTS public."order";

CREATE TABLE IF NOT EXISTS public."order"
(
    id integer NOT NULL DEFAULT
nextval('order_id_seq'::regclass),
    "userId" integer,
    "orderDate" date,
    items character varying COLLATE
pg_catalog."default",
    total numeric,
    "labelUrl" character varying COLLATE
pg_catalog."default",
    "trackingNumber" character varying COLLATE
pg_catalog."default",
    "trackingUrl" character varying COLLATE
pg_catalog."default",
    "transObjId" character varying STORAGE
PLAIN COLLATE pg_catalog."default",
    "paymentIntentId" character varying STORAGE
PLAIN COLLATE pg_catalog."default",
    "summaryId" integer,
    CONSTRAINT order_pkey PRIMARY KEY (id)
)

TABLESPACE pg_default;

ALTER TABLE IF EXISTS public."order"
    OWNER to shrova_admin;
```

order_summary

```
-- Table: public.order_summary

-- DROP TABLE IF EXISTS public.order_summary;

CREATE TABLE IF NOT EXISTS public.order_summary
(
    id integer NOT NULL DEFAULT
nextval('order_summary_id_seq'::regclass),
    "userId" integer,
    "orderDate" date,
    items character varying COLLATE
pg_catalog."default",
    total numeric,
    "rateId" character varying STORAGE PLAIN
COLLATE pg_catalog."default",
    CONSTRAINT order_summary_pkey PRIMARY KEY
(id)
)

TABLESPACE pg_default;

ALTER TABLE IF EXISTS public.order_summary
    OWNER to shrova_admin;
```

payment_intent

```
-- Table: public.payment_intent

-- DROP TABLE IF EXISTS public.payment_intent;

CREATE TABLE IF NOT EXISTS
public.payment_intent
```

```sql
(
    id integer NOT NULL DEFAULT
nextval('payment_intent_id_seq'::regclass),
    "paymentIntentId" character varying COLLATE
pg_catalog."default",
    "userId" integer,
    "summaryId" integer,
    CONSTRAINT payment_intent_pkey PRIMARY KEY
(id)
)

TABLESPACE pg_default;

ALTER TABLE IF EXISTS public.payment_intent
    OWNER to shrova_admin;
```

product

```sql
-- Table: public.product

-- DROP TABLE IF EXISTS public.product;

CREATE TABLE IF NOT EXISTS public.product
(
    id integer NOT NULL DEFAULT
nextval('product_id_seq'::regclass),
    title character varying COLLATE
pg_catalog."default",
    description character varying COLLATE
pg_catalog."default",
    category integer,
    "imageUrl" character varying COLLATE
pg_catalog."default",
    published boolean,
```

```sql
    price numeric,
    stock integer,
    length integer,
    width integer,
    height integer,
    "distanceUnit" character varying COLLATE
pg_catalog."default",
    weight integer,
    "massUnit" character varying COLLATE
pg_catalog."default",
    CONSTRAINT product_pkey PRIMARY KEY (id)
)

TABLESPACE pg_default;

ALTER TABLE IF EXISTS public.product
    OWNER to shrova_admin;
```

store_settings

```sql
-- Table: public.store_settings

-- DROP TABLE IF EXISTS public.store_settings;

CREATE TABLE IF NOT EXISTS
public.store_settings
(
    id integer NOT NULL DEFAULT
nextval('store_settings_id_seq'::regclass),
    "storeName" character varying COLLATE
pg_catalog."default",
    street1 character varying COLLATE
pg_catalog."default",
```

```sql
    city character varying COLLATE
pg_catalog."default",
    state character varying COLLATE
pg_catalog."default",
    zip character varying COLLATE
pg_catalog."default",
    country character varying COLLATE
pg_catalog."default",
    CONSTRAINT store_settings_pkey PRIMARY KEY
(id)
)

TABLESPACE pg_default;

ALTER TABLE IF EXISTS public.store_settings
    OWNER to shrova_admin;
```

user

```sql
-- Table: public.user

-- DROP TABLE IF EXISTS public."user";

CREATE TABLE IF NOT EXISTS public."user"
(
    id integer NOT NULL DEFAULT
nextval('user_id_seq'::regclass),
    firstname character varying COLLATE
pg_catalog."default",
    lastname character varying COLLATE
pg_catalog."default",
    email character varying COLLATE
pg_catalog."default",
```

```
    password character varying COLLATE
pg_catalog."default",
    "resetPasswordToken" character varying
COLLATE pg_catalog."default",
    "tokenCreatedAt" timestamp without time
zone,
    "isAdmin" boolean,
    CONSTRAINT user_pkey PRIMARY KEY (id)
)

TABLESPACE pg_default;

ALTER TABLE IF EXISTS public."user"
    OWNER to shrova_admin;
```

Development Steps

1. The first step is to install NestJS on your computer.
    - First download and install NodeJS.
    - Install Nest cli.
2. Create a new Nest project called shrova-be.
3. Create a new GitHub repository called shrova-be.
4. Connect your local project to the online GitHub repository.
    - When we are done with the changes on our local machine, we push them to the remote GitHub repository.
5. To deploy our application, we'll create a new web service on render.com

- Connect the new web service to the GitHub repository shrova-be.
    - Every time we push updates to the repository, render.com will automatically put it online.
6. Add environment variables to the web service on render.com and we are done with the backend development.

Our backend server is now ready to serve the frontend application.

Now we can move on to the final step: developing the frontend application.

These were the development steps we needed to take to get our application up and running.
Throughout the book, we'll see how to achieve each step in detail.

So, let's get started.

Install NestJS

If this is the first time to work with NestJS, you need to install the following applications
1. Download and install NodeJS
2. Download and install Visual Studio Code
3. Install NestJS CLI
   Open the terminal and execute the command

```
npm install -g @nestjs/cli
```

Create new project

Create the nestjs project **shrova-be** on your local
machine as follows, execute the command
```
nest new shrova-be
```

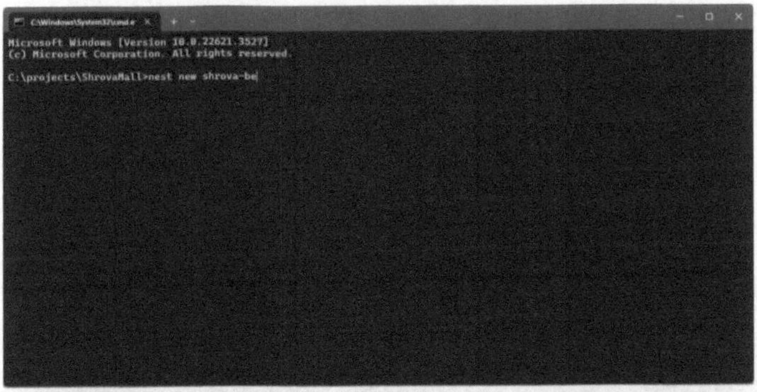

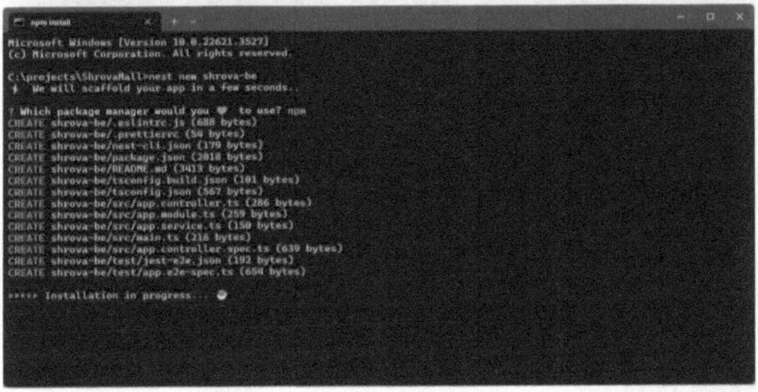

```
C:\Windows\System32\cmd.e    ×    +  ∨                            –   □   ×
Microsoft Windows [Version 10.0.22621.3527]
(c) Microsoft Corporation. All rights reserved.

C:\projects\ShrovaMall>nest new shrova-be
```

```
npm install                  ×    +  ∨                            –   □   ×
Microsoft Windows [Version 10.0.22621.3527]
(c) Microsoft Corporation. All rights reserved.

C:\projects\ShrovaMall>nest new shrova-be
⚡  We will scaffold your app in a few seconds..

? Which package manager would you ♥  to use? npm
CREATE shrova-be/.eslintrc.js (688 bytes)
CREATE shrova-be/.prettierrc (54 bytes)
CREATE shrova-be/nest-cli.json (179 bytes)
CREATE shrova-be/package.json (2018 bytes)
CREATE shrova-be/README.md (3413 bytes)
CREATE shrova-be/tsconfig.build.json (101 bytes)
CREATE shrova-be/tsconfig.json (567 bytes)
CREATE shrova-be/src/app.controller.ts (286 bytes)
CREATE shrova-be/src/app.module.ts (259 bytes)
CREATE shrova-be/src/app.service.ts (150 bytes)
CREATE shrova-be/src/main.ts (216 bytes)
CREATE shrova-be/src/app.controller.spec.ts (639 bytes)
CREATE shrova-be/test/jest-e2e.json (192 bytes)
CREATE shrova-be/test/app.e2e-spec.ts (654 bytes)

▸▸▸▸▸ Installation in progress... ●
```

Open the project in Visual Studio Code. From the file menu choose "Open Folder" and open the project as follows

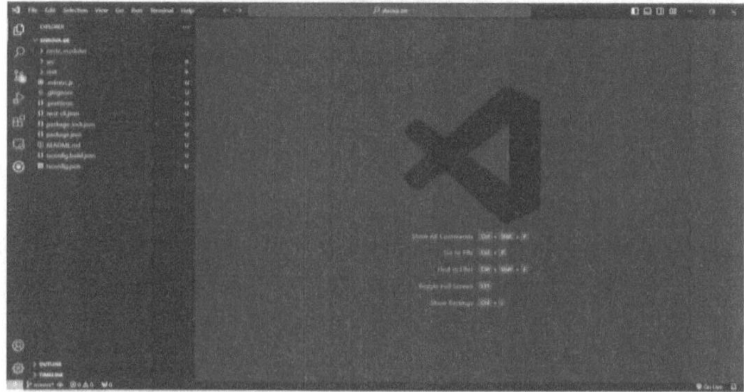

Create new repository on GitHub

Login to your GitHub account or create one if you don't have one already.

Create a new repository **shrova-be** for the backend
project as follows

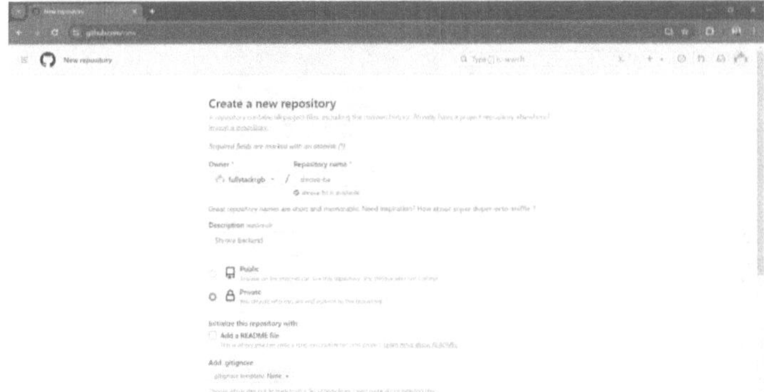

Setup SSH

To be able to connect to GitHub and push code from
your local machine, you need to set up SSH keys.

Generate the SSH Key on your machine first and then
add it to GitHub.

Install Git Bash on your machine if you haven't done it
already

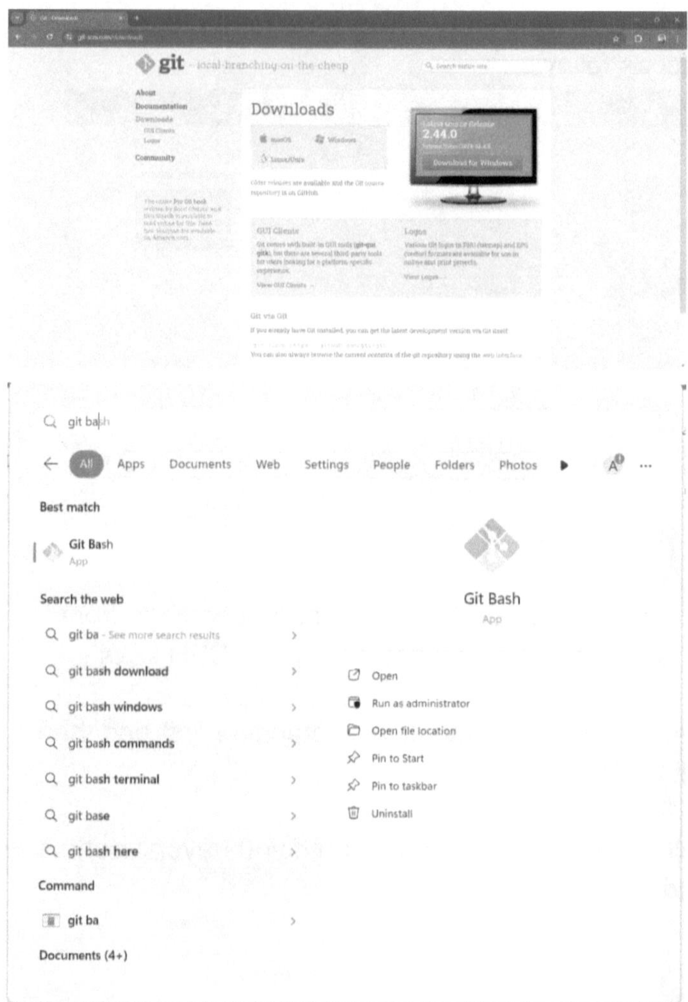

To generate a new SSH Key, open Git Bash and
execute the following command

```
ssh-keygen -t ed25519 -C "your_email"
```

Use your email of course.

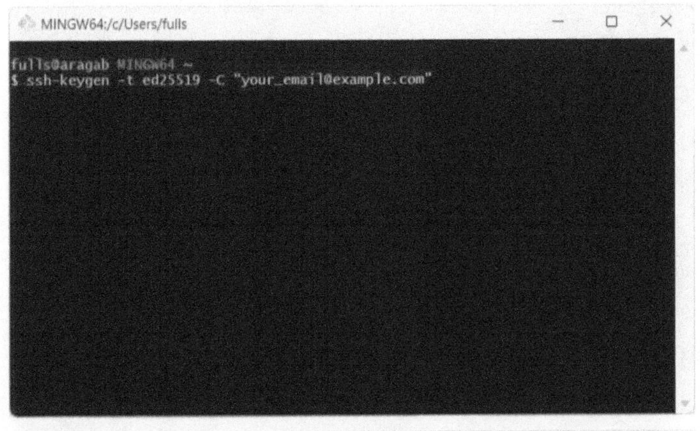

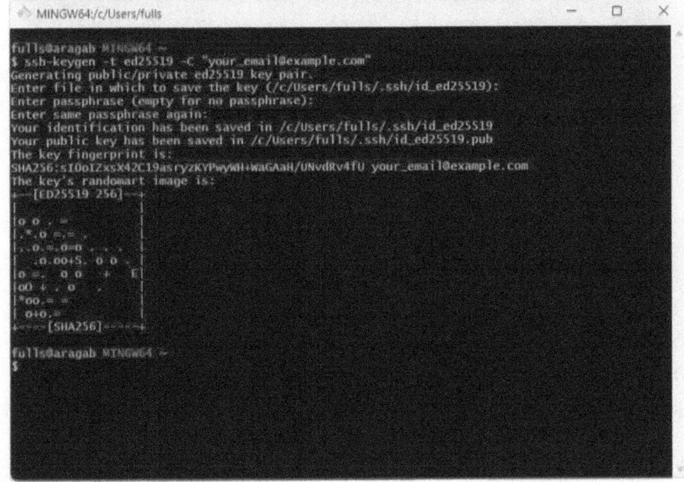

Open the .pub file in the notepad and copy all contents

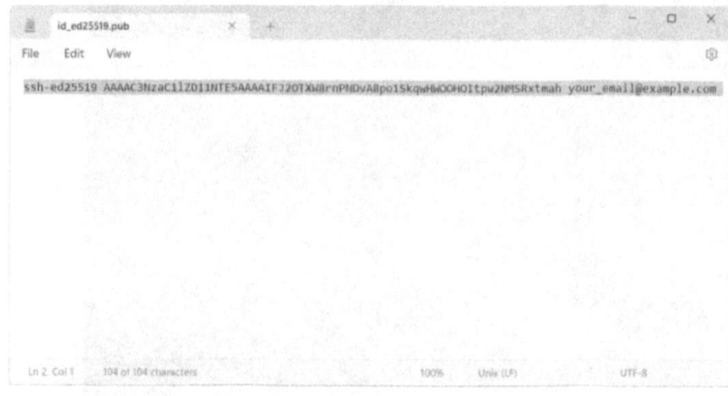

Go to the GitHub website and "Settings" → "SSH Keys"
→ "New SSH Key"

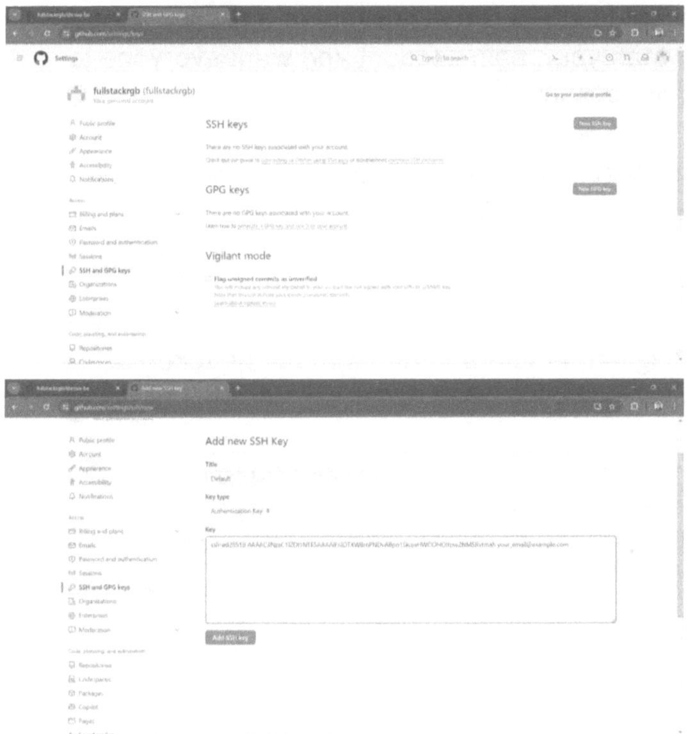

Now your machine is connected to your online GitHub account.

Personal Access Tokens

Another option, if you don't want to add SSH keys to your machine, is to create a personal access token and add it to the URL of the remote repository. This way, you can authorize repositories individually and easily connect to many GitHub accounts. This can be useful if you want to connect a repository to a GitHub account other than your main account and want everyone to work at the same time.

Personal access tokens is attached to the remote repository address like this
`https://`**`ghp_UWKEScKNTrSwZiBlJP419ruYhyOuRS2Ucp`**
`Vp``@github.com/fullstackrgb/shrova-be.git`

The original remote address without the token is
`https://github.com/fullstackrgb/shrova-be.git`

To create a personal access token go to the developer settings at the end of the settings page

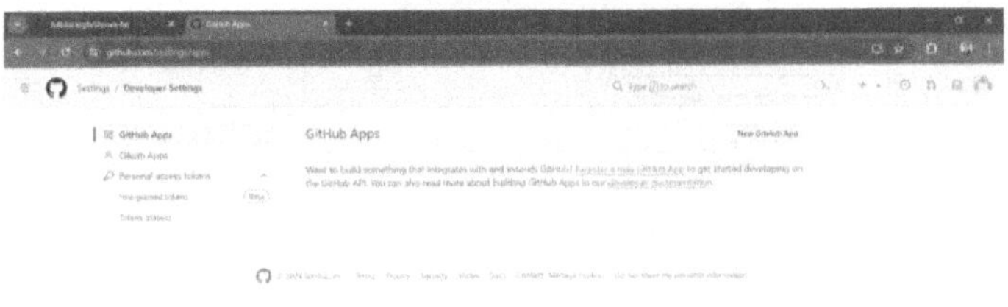
Settings / Developer Settings
GitHub Apps
New GitHub App

New personal access token (classic)
Note
Expiration
Select scopes
repo
workflow
Settings / Developer Settings
Personal access tokens (classic)
Tokens you have generated that can be used to access the GitHub API.
Make sure to copy your personal access tokens now. You won't be able to see it again!

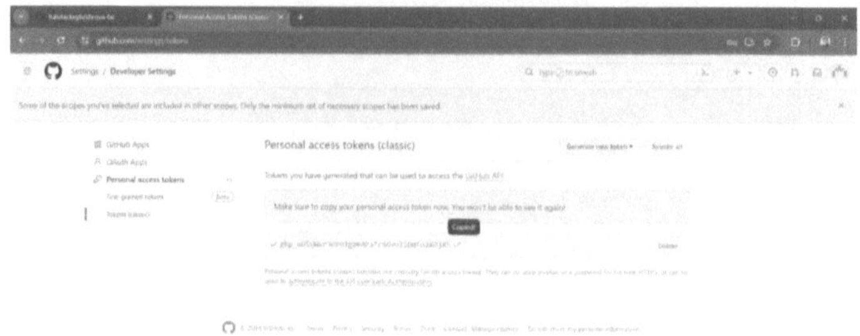

We will connect the local repository to the remote
repository soon and to do so we will use the following
command:

```
git remote add origin
https://github.com/fullstackrgb/shrova-b
e.git
```

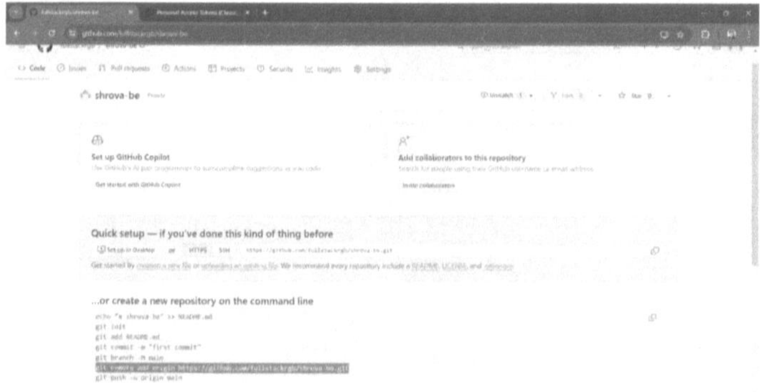

Now add the token to the origin url as follows

```
git remote add origin
https://here_followed_by_@github.com/fullstackr
gb/shrova-be.git
```

```
git remote add origin
https://ghp_uO5UWwrJ6P91g0K4PaTcSdvoIIDmfo2X0jX
5@github.com/fullstackrgb/shrova-be.git
```

Both ways work well and you are free to choose what
works best for you.

Connect to your GitHub repository

Open the Visual Studio Code terminal

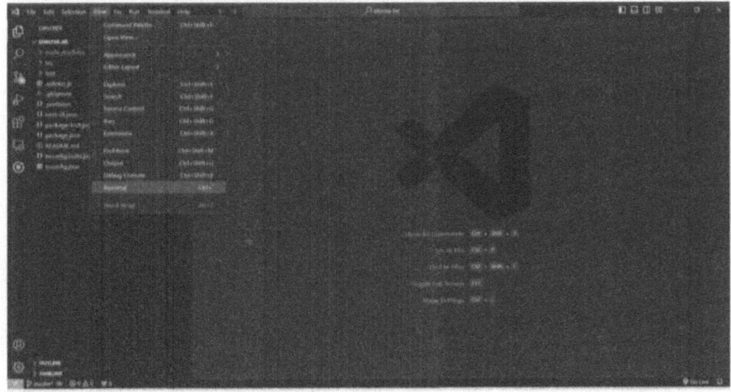

Execute the commands:
```
git add .
```

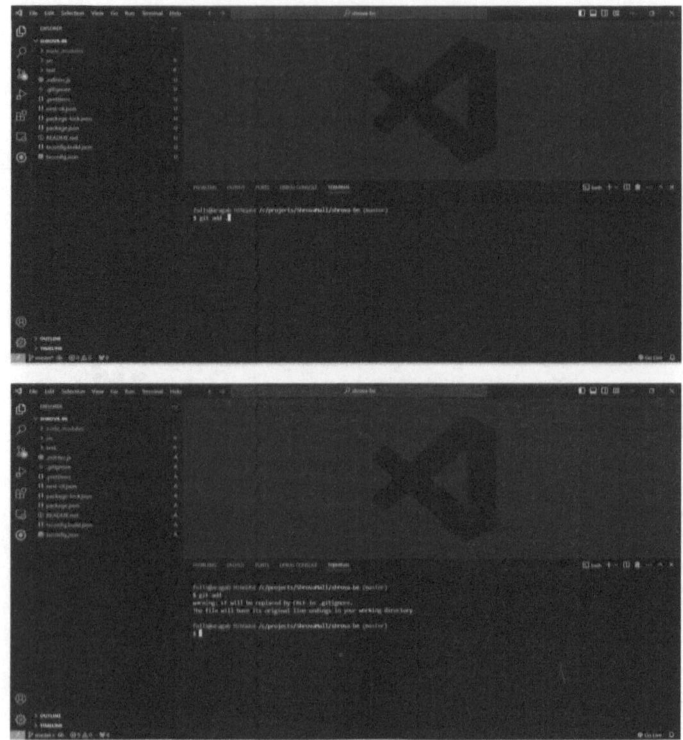

git commit -m "Initial"

git branch -M main

git remote add origin
https://ghp_uO5UWwrJ6P91g0K4PaTcSdvoIIDmfo2X0jX
5@github.com/fullstackrgb/shrova-be.git

git push -u origin main

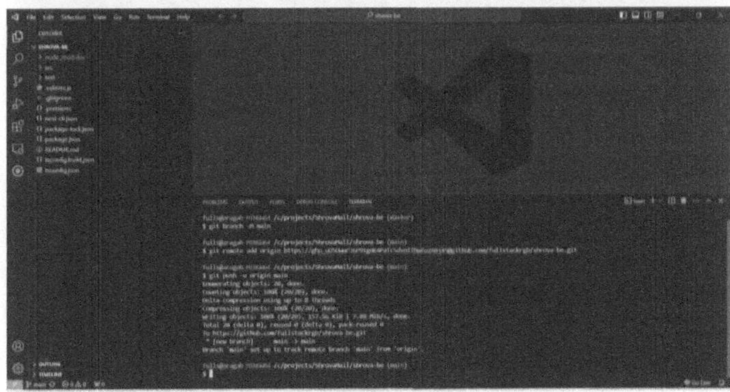

Note: To clear the terminal use the command `clear` *for Git Bash and* `cls` *for the Command Prompt*

This was the page when you created the repo

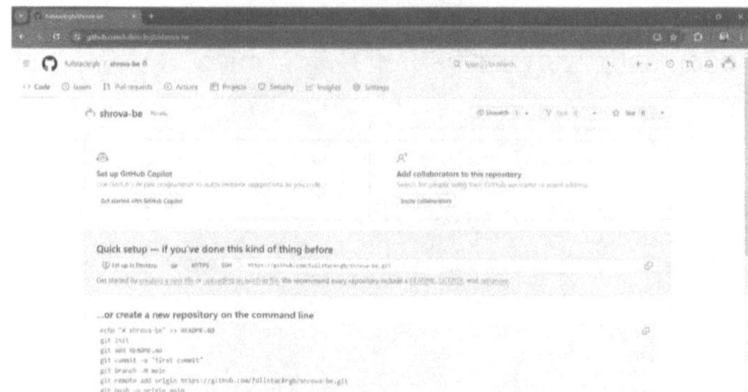

If you visit it now, you will find your code posted online

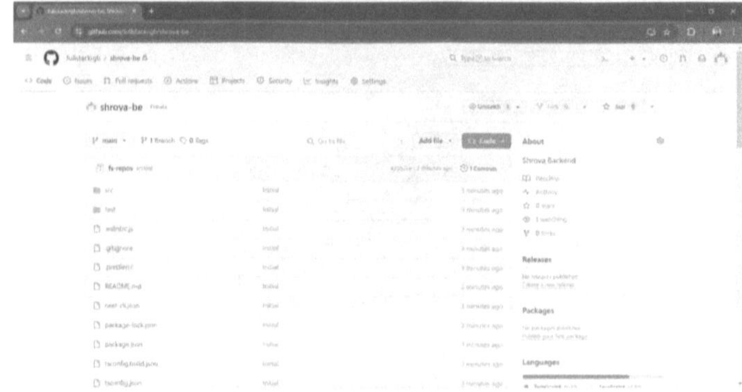

When you want to push modifications online, you can execute the commands:

```
git add .
git commit -m "update message"
git push
```

Disable .eslintrc.js

After I have created the application, I delete everything in the **.eslintrc.js** because it reports unnecessary errors. Remove everything from the **.eslintrc.js** file and keep an empty object as follows
module.exports = {};

Now do a Developer: Reload Window from the command palette. You can reach it from the View menu or by pressing CTRL + SHIFT + P

Configure App in Main.ts

Next, you need to activate cors and activate both raw and body parsers.
The raw parser is required to accept external requests from various providers such as Stripe.

Update the **main.ts** file as follows:

```typescript
import { NestFactory } from '@nestjs/core';
import { AppModule } from './app.module';

async function bootstrap() {
  const app = await
NestFactory.create(AppModule, {
    bodyParser: true,
    rawBody: true,
  });
  app.enableCors();
  await app.listen(3000);
}
bootstrap();
```

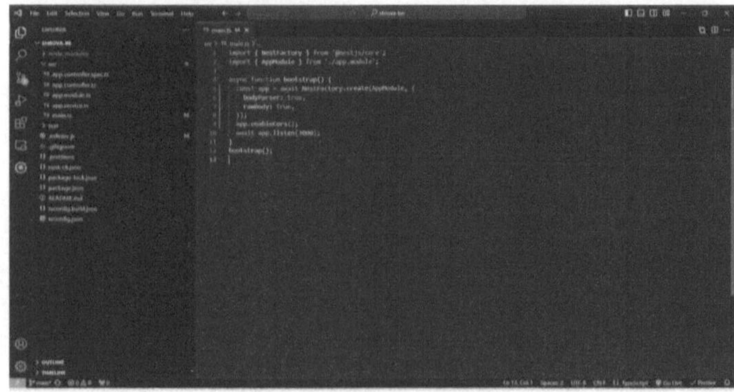

Install Dependencies

Here is a list of all the dependencies we will be using:
- @nestjs/typeorm
- typeorm
- pg
- class-transformer
- class-validator

- dotenv
- nodemailer
- @nestjs/jwt
- @nestjs/passport
- passport
- passport-jwt
- passport-local
- shippo
- stripe

1. `@nestjs/typeorm, typeorm` **and** `pg` are used to manipulate the database schema and perform operations such as reading and saving in the database.

   Although typeorm can be used to manipulate the database schema and create the database tables and columns based on the entity definitions, I will not use this in our application. You should make the changes yourself on the database server to avoid data loss. For this reason, I have set sync to false to disable database manipulation by typeorm.
   We will instead use pgAdmin on the database server when we want to make changes to the database, and you've already seen that (for more information, see the second book, Shrova Mall 2 - The Database).

2. The `class-validator` package supports the validation of data, while the

`class-transformer` package enables the transformation of data.
3. `dotenv` is a zero-dependency module that loads environment variables from a **.env** file into process.env
4. `nodemailer` sends emails from Node.js
5. `@nestjs/jwt, @nestjs/passport, passport, passport-jwt, passport-local` the most popular node.js authentication library
6. `shippo` is a shipping API that connects you with multiple shipping carriers (such as USPS, UPS, DHL, and many others) through one interface.
7. `stripe` provides convenient access to the Stripe API

Install the dependencies by executing the command:
```
npm install @nestjs/typeorm typeorm pg
class-transformer class-validator dotenv
nodemailer @nestjs/jwt @nestjs/passport
passport passport-jwt passport-local shippo
stripe
```

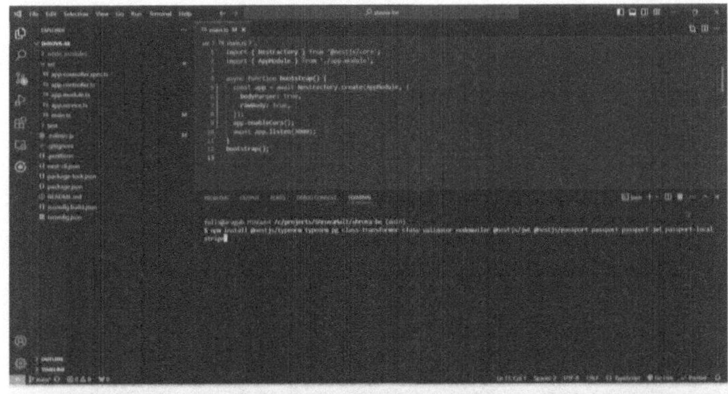

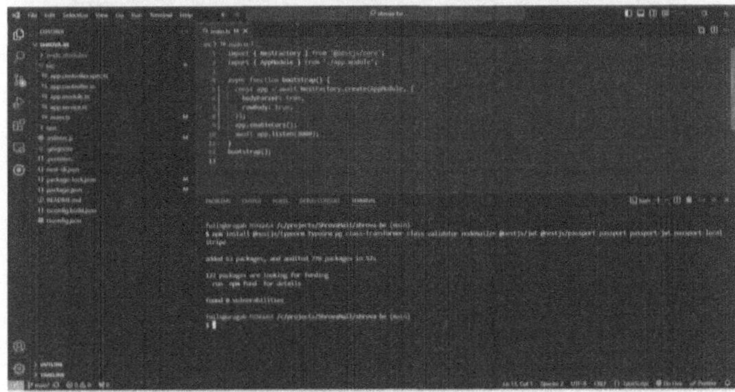

Environment Variables

Create a .env file and paste the following configuration.

```
STRIPE_SECRET_KEY=placeholder
STRIPE_WEBHOOK_SECRET_KEY=placeholder
POSTGRES_DATABASE=placeholder
POSTGRES_HOST=placeholder
POSTGRES_PASSWORD=placeholder
POSTGRES_PORT=placeholder
POSTGRES_SSL=placeholder
POSTGRES_USER=placeholder
```

```
JWT_SECRET=placeholder
MAILER_SERVICE=placeholder
MAILER_HOST=placeholder
MAILER_PORT=placeholder
MAILER_SECURE=placeholder
MAILER_EMAIL=placeholder
MAILER_PASSWORD=placeholder
```

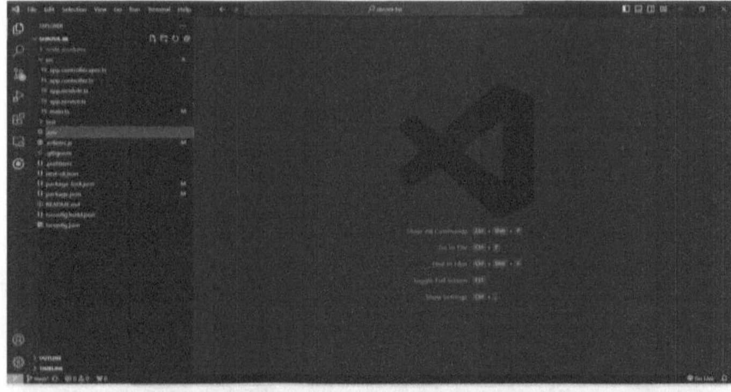

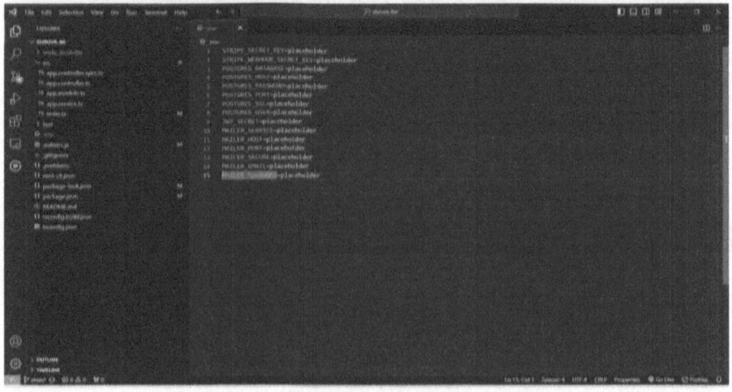

These environment variables are used with our application while we are in development. When we publish the application online, the server's variables will be used instead.

Connect to the Database

Update app.module.ts as follows:

```
import { config } from 'dotenv';
config();
```

Import the TypeOrmModule.forRoot with the following configuration.

```
    TypeOrmModule.forRoot({
      type: 'postgres',
      host: `${process.env.POSTGRES_HOST}`,
      port: +`${process.env.POSTGRES_PORT}`,
      username: `${process.env.POSTGRES_USER}`,
      password:
`${process.env.POSTGRES_PASSWORD}`,
      database:
`${process.env.POSTGRES_DATABASE}`,
      entities: [__dirname +
'/**/*.entity.{ts,js}'],
      ssl:
`${process.env.POSTGRES_SSL}`.toLowerCase() ==
'true',
      synchronize: false,
    }),
```

Always set synchronization to false when connecting to the production database.

This is what the app.module.ts looks like now

```
import { Module } from '@nestjs/common';
import { AppController } from
'./app.controller';
import { AppService } from './app.service';
```

```typescript
import { TypeOrmModule } from
'@nestjs/typeorm';
import { config } from 'dotenv';
config();

@Module({
  imports: [
    TypeOrmModule.forRoot({
      type: 'postgres',
      host: `${process.env.POSTGRES_HOST}`,
      port: +`${process.env.POSTGRES_PORT}`,
      username: `${process.env.POSTGRES_USER}`,
      password:
`${process.env.POSTGRES_PASSWORD}`,
      database:
`${process.env.POSTGRES_DATABASE}`,
      entities: [__dirname +
'/**/*.entity.{ts,js}'],
      ssl:
`${process.env.POSTGRES_SSL}`.toLowerCase() ==
'true',
      synchronize: false,
    }),
  ],
  controllers: [AppController],
  providers: [AppService],
})
export class AppModule {}
```

For the database connection values in the .env file

```
POSTGRES_DATABASE=placeholder
POSTGRES_HOST=placeholder
POSTGRES_PASSWORD=placeholder
POSTGRES_PORT=placeholder
```

```
POSTGRES_SSL=placeholder
POSTGRES_USER=placeholder
```

Replace placeholder with the intended values. You can get the values from the database info page on Render.com

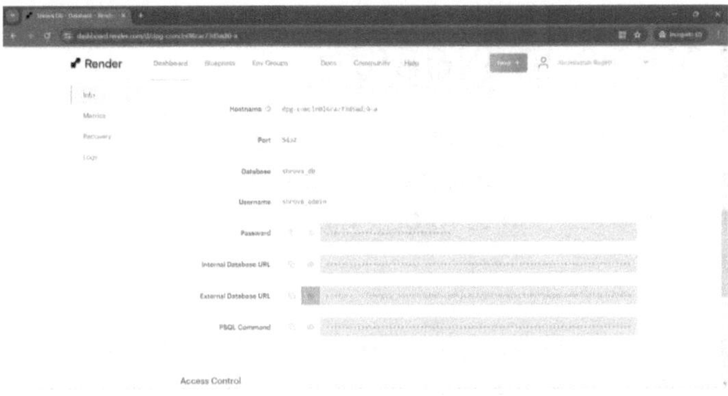

```
POSTGRES_DATABASE=shrova_db
POSTGRES_HOST=dpg-comcln016cac73d5adi0-a.orego
n-postgres.render.com
POSTGRES_PASSWORD=*************************
POSTGRES_PORT=5432
POSTGRES_SSL=true
POSTGRES_USER=shrova_admin
```

Later, we will create new environment variables for the backend service on the Render.com server that are different from the ones we are using now on our local machine.
When we deploy the application to Render.com, these values will be used on the server.

We will also use the short hostname and set SSL to false as the connection will be within the private Render.com network. However, nothing will change in the code, only the online environment variables will be different.

Modules in NestJS

A module is a class annotated with a @Module() decorator. The @Module() decorator provides metadata that Nest makes use of to organize the application structure.

Each application has at least one module, a root module. Modules are strongly recommended as an effective way to organize your components. Thus, for most applications, the resulting architecture will employ multiple modules, each encapsulating a closely related set of capabilities.

To create a module in NestJS, you can use the `nest generate module moduleName` command.
After you have created the module, you can create services, controllers and so on.
You can create them all together with the `nest generate resource resourceName` command.

For example the cart module consists of:
```
src
└── core
```

```
└── cart
    ├── cart.controller.ts
    ├── cart.entity.ts
    ├── cart.module.ts
    └── cart.service.ts
```

Application Modules

Here is a list of all the modules we will create in our application:

- auth
- cart
- categories
- mailer
- newsletter
- orders
- products
- shippo
- storage
- store-settings
- stripe
- users

auth

The auth module is responsible for all associated authentication processes such as login, registration and validation of requests.

The typical authentication scenario begins with the user registering a new account. After adding the new user to the database, we ask jwt to give the user a new access token, which is returned in the response.
At the frontend, we receive the token and store it in localStorage. Using the http_interceptor, we add it to all subsequent http requests.

When the server receives subsequent requests, it looks for the token in the header, validates it and checks that it has not expired.

When a user tries to log in, we search the database for the username and password. When we find them, we ask jwt to issue an access token to the user and return it in the response. And the same scenario continues here.

JWT uses three different strategies to accomplish this. First, it uses the local strategy when the user enters the username and password. So we need to implement the validate method and tell jwt whether the username and password are correct or not. Based on this, jwt decides whether it should issue an access token.

The second strategy is the jwt strategy, which checks whether a request should be provided with an access token.

In the first strategy, the local strategy, there are therefore no access tokens, only the user name and password, which should generate an access token when they are passed.

In the second strategy, the jwt strategy, the system checks whether the access token from the last step, the local strategy, is valid and has not expired.

There is a third strategy that you can use or not: the refresh strategy. We use it in the application, so let me explain it to you.

The jwt access token should have a validity period and it should be short.

However, when the jwt token expires, the user is prompted to log in again. So if I decide that the jwt token expires after 5 minutes, the user has to log in again every 5 minutes, which is very annoying. And if I set the validity period to 1 hour, you run the risk of being hacked.

This is where the refresh strategy fills the gap.
The refresh strategy can have a long validity period, e.g. 7 days, so that you can generate a refresh token every 7 days. If you have set up the refresh strategy, you can set the expiry of the jwt token to a short period of time, e.g. 5 minutes.

If you activate the refresh strategy and authenticate with the local strategy for the first time, you will receive two tokens instead of one.

You will receive the access token, which expires after 5 minutes, and a refresh token, which is valid for 7 days and both of which you must save in the local strategy.

In the http_interceptor we change this a bit: We still add the access tokens to the header of all requests, nothing changes. But we check all responses for the 401 Unauthorized response. If we find it, we send the refresh token to the backend and ask for a new access token. The backend issues a new access token based on the refresh token and sends it back to the frontend. Without terminating the currently executing method, we retry the last failed unauthorized request after replacing the old token with the new token and refresh the local storage to use the new token for all subsequent requests.

This process continues as long as the user continues to use the application. We have a new token every 5 minutes, repeat the last failed unauthorized request and update the tokens.

This way we achieve the highest level of security and a good user experience, because now the user can stay logged in for 7 days, but we issue new tokens every 5 minutes.

In the authModule definition in the imports array, you will find the jwt `expiresIn` set to 5 minutes or 300 seconds ('300s')

```
JwtModule.register({
    secret: `${process.env.JWT_SECRET}`,
    signOptions: { expiresIn: '300s' },
  }),
```

In the authService, when we create the refresh token in
the login method, we set its expiration time to 7 days
('7d') as follows:

```
  async login(user: User) {
   ...
    return {
      ...
      refreshToken:
this.jwtService.sign(payload, { expiresIn: '7d'
}),
      ...
    };
  }
```

Passwords are encrypted

Now that you know how authentication works, there are
two more details you need to know about the
authentication module.

The first is that we store the passwords encrypted in the
database, using irreversible encryption techniques.
This protects customer' data in case the database is
hacked. Usually, customers use the same password for
many websites, and if it is exposed, it will affect all their
accounts on many other platforms.

When encrypting the password, we generate a random
encryption key each time, which is different for each
password. We append it to the end of the encrypted
password, put a dot in between and store it in the
database so that we can later use the same encryption
key to verify login attempts.

By encrypting our customer' passwords, nobody can find
out the original password, not even us.

If the user tries to log in again later, we first retrieve the
encrypted password from the database and the
encryption key.

We simply repeat the same encryption process with the
password entered, using the same encryption key we
just extracted, and compare the results. If the two
results match, i.e. the old password stored in the
database and the encryption result for the newly entered
password, then the password is correct and should be
accepted, otherwise it is incorrect and the user will
receive an error message indicating the incorrect
password.

Reset password

The second thing you need to know is how we reset the
password in our application, and here's how.

When the user clicks on "Forgot password" in the front-end application, they are redirected to a page where they can enter their email address.

Once it has been sent to the backend, we first check whether a user with this e-mail address is stored in our database. If we do not find it, we report an error message that there is no such user in our system.

If there is already a user with the specified email address in the database, we start the password reset process.
First, we create a reset token and store it in the user table in the database in the resetPasswordToken field and store the time it was created in the tokenCreatedAt field.

Then we create a new link with the token and the attached user email and add it to the reset email message.
Using the Nodemailer module, we send the message to the specified email address.

When the user clicks on the link in the message, he/she is redirected to a new page in the frontend application where he/she can enter a new password.

When the user enters the new password, we compare the associated token with the token in the user table. The values must match and the time window must not be longer than one hour, otherwise it is considered expired and the user must start the process from the beginning.

If it is accepted, we encrypt the newly entered password and save the result in the user table in the password field. We can then delete the values in the resetPasswordToken and tokenCreatedAt fields.

Endpoints

The auth controller has five endpoints for login, register, refresh, request-reset-password, and reset-password. The login endpoint is protected with a LocalAuthGuard. The login endpoint is guarded with a LocalAuthGuard. This means that the execution of the validate method of the local strategy is enforced by jwt.

We have three guards and three strategies:
1. We have a local auth guard and a local strategy.
2. We have a jwt auth guard and a jwt strategy.
3. And finally, we have a jwt refresh auth guard and a jwt refresh strategy.

We should apply the appropriate protection measure at each execution point of the application.

For example, the registration endpoint, which we will explain in a moment, should not have any guards at all, as it is the entry point into the application and should not be protected. Anyone should be able to register without further checks.

We apply the LocalAuthGuard to the login method, because to get to the login method, you must first enter a valid username and password, otherwise you will not be allowed to reach the login method.

If the validation is successful, the current user object is attached to the request object so that all future methods dealing with the request object can read it. You just need to call it as follows: request.user

For the rest of our application, we use the JwtGuard, which checks the incoming request for the access token and verifies that it is valid before allowing you to access the desired method.

As mentioned earlier, we use the LocalAuthGuard for the login, and that's the only place we need to use it.

The registration endpoint has no protection mechanisms. It first checks whether the specified email address is not already registered for another user.
A new user is then created and saved in the database.
In the last step, the user is automatically logged in by calling up the login method with the specified user name and password.

The refresh endpoint is responsible for issuing a new access token when the old one has expired.
It is guarded by a RefreshJwtGuard.

When we call the refresh endpoint from the frontend, we pass the refresh token in the request body, which is received in the backend and extracted from the request body.
Once extracted and confirmed as true, the logic in the RefreshPoint method is executed where we ask the jwtService to re-sign the user, resulting in a new access token.

```
@UseGuards(RefreshJwtGuard)
@Post('refresh')
async refrshToken(@Request() req) {
  return
this.authService.refreshToken(req.user);
  }
```

The request-reset-password endpoint sends a password reset message to the user's email address.
In the message sent, we embed the token, the email and all the details required for the reset process.

For the reset-password endpoint, we receive the new password from the frontend and it should contain the security token that was appended to the last endpoint's request.
They should match within an hour. So we can go ahead and update the user's password to the new password.

cart

The shopping cart module is responsible for saving the status of the shopping cart at all times.

It saves the status as a string. The front-end application is responsible for converting to and from the string.
It has two endpoints for reading and saving state, without any route paths, just the method types.

categories

The Categories module is responsible for obtaining information about the categories. It has two endpoints, one to retrieve all categories and one to retrieve a category by its ID.
I manually entered the categories directly into the database.
In addition to the ID and title, the category entity has two other columns, one for the parentId to manage the parent-child relationship and another field for the order to determine in which order the categories should be displayed.

mailer

The mailer module is responsible for sending emails from our application, currently we use it for sending password reset email messages. It has no endpoints, we only need the mailer service.

newsletter

The newsletter module is a completely independent module and is not related to any other module in the system. It has two endpoints to accept subscription emails and another to unsubscribe.

orders

The order module is responsible for managing the online store's orders at different phases. It has two main entities, the OrderSummary entity and the Order entity. The OrderSummary entity is used to track the order as long as it has not yet been completed. Once the order is completed, a new Order object is created and stored in the database.

There are three endpoints to creating an order summary, receiving all orders, and receiving an order by ID.

Keep in mind a general rule that we apply in our system. When we call a get all method, we should pass two parameters: take and skip. Since we use pagination in our system, we only get the records for the current page. You must never retrieve all records from the database without pagination parameters. The only exception is categories, where we return all records because it makes no sense to paginate categories as we want to have all records no matter how big they are, and they are by nature limited to a small number of records by the way.

products

The product module is responsible for managing all product-related details. There are many endpoints in the product controller and most of them are similar. They are variations on how you can retrieve products. Sometimes you want all products in a certain category, sometimes you want to filter all products by certain criteria and so on. In addition to the endpoints for retrieving products, there are endpoints for calculating shipping costs, for checkout and of course an endpoint for adding a new product via the administration page.

Endpoints

The Product Controller has many endpoints to query products from the database.
In addition to the product queries, there are endpoints for creating new products, querying shipping costs and carrying out the checkout process.

The endpoints for querying shipping rates use the Shippo service from the Shippo module to get a list of all available rates. We need to pass addressFrom, addressTo and the packages we want to ship.

After the user has selected a suitable shipping rate, we save the selected rate number to use it later for calculating the total price by adding the shipping charges and creating the shipping label.

For the checkout we use the Stripe module. The checkout method uses the Stripe SDK to create a new checkout session and pass it to the Frotend application, which initiates the payment process.

We have already set up webhooks for Stripe events so that we are notified as soon as the payment is completed.

We are interested in two events, the "checkout.session.completed" event and the "payment_intent.succeeded" event.
We receive the former when the user starts the payment process, so Stripe sends us the paymentIntentId.

If the payment was successful and the money was credited to your Stripe account, you will receive a notification via the "payment_intent.succeeded" event.

Now the order is completed and you can create a new order object and save it in the database with all details about the products, the total amount, the shipping label, the tracking url and tracking number as well as all necessary details.

We also empty the shopping cart in the database to prepare it for new orders.

shippo

The purpose of the shippo module is to support the shipping of products by using the shippo sdk.
The shippo service has three main methods: getRates to get all shipping options based on the given addresses and packages, getRate to get the details of a specific shipping rate based on its ID, and createTransaction to create the shipping label for the given rateId.

storage

We use the storage module to upload images to the Firebase storage. It has only one endpoint, which accepts the file to be uploaded and uploads it to the Firebase storage.

store-settings

The store has two basic settings, the store name and the store address. The store name is displayed as the brand name and the address is used to ship products to customers. The store settings module is responsible for saving and reading the store settings from the database and has a store settings entity alongside the service and the controller.

stripe

The stripe module has two main tasks: It intercepts the webhook events and manipulates the payment intent objects.
When the checkout session starts, Stripe sends us a payment intent object in the webhook event, which we store in the database.
Once the payment is completed, we receive another webhook event telling us that the payment has been completed.

user

The user module takes care of the user entity and two other entities, the address and the default_address.
Each user has many addresses for shipping and billing and can decide which one to use by default.
We store the addresses in the addresses table and the default addresses in the default_address table.

Debug

To start the application execute the command `nest start`.
To display the executed sql query, update the app.module.ts in the import of TypeOrmModule.forRoot({ by adding the **logging: true**.

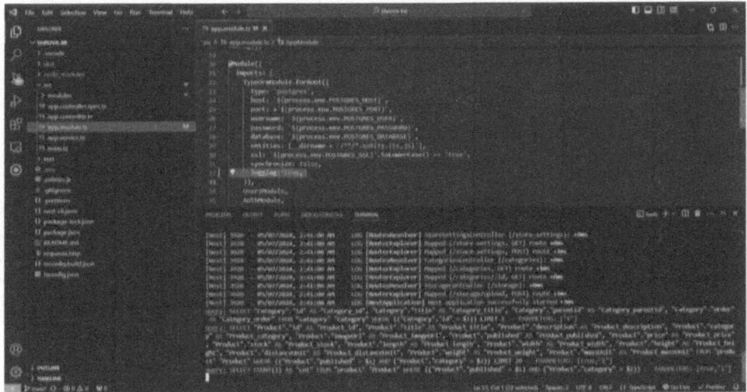

The executed queries are displayed in the console, as you can see.

If you want to set a breakpoint to stop the execution of the application at a certain point and check the variables and the call stack etc., you can do so as follows:
Create a new folder ".vscode" at the root of the project.
Create a new file launch.json inside the ".vscode" folder and add the following code to it:

```json
{
    "version": "0.2.0",
    "configurations": [
        {
            "type": "node",
            "request": "launch",
            "name": "Debug Nest Framework",
            "args":
["${workspaceFolder}/src/main.ts"],
            "runtimeArgs": [
                "--nolazy",
                "-r",
                "ts-node/register",
```

```json
        "-r",
        "tsconfig-paths/register"
      ],
      "sourceMaps": true,
      "envFile": "${workspaceFolder}/.env",
      "cwd": "${workspaceRoot}",
      "console": "integratedTerminal",
      "protocol": "inspector"
    }
  ]
}
```

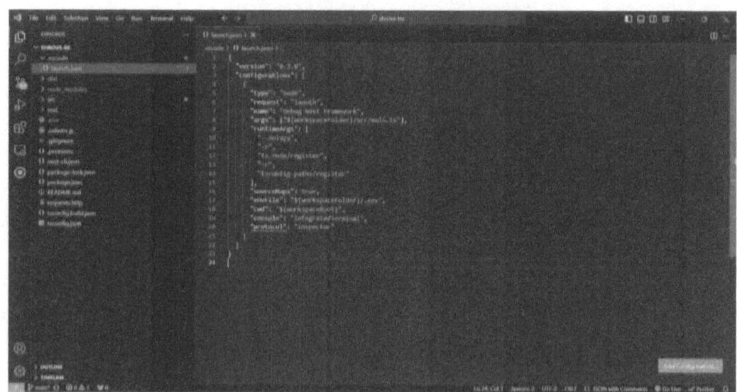

Make sure that you terminate the running Nest program in the terminal.
Set a breakpoint at the point where you want to stop execution and start debugging.

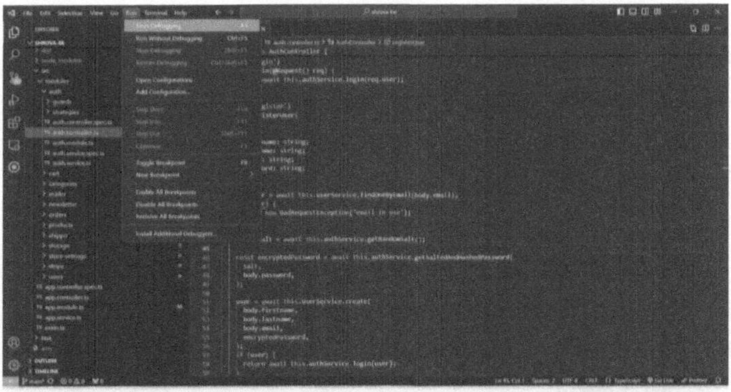

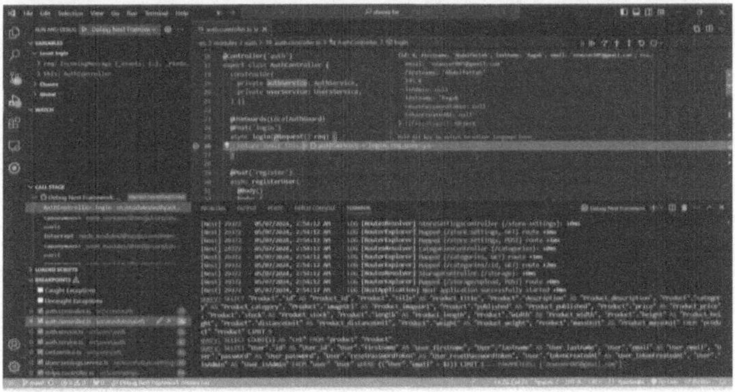

Deployment

As you know, we use render.com for hosting. We have already published the database in the second book of the series (Shrova Mall 2 - The Database).
Now we will also publish the backend on Render.com. Deployment on render.com is very simple. First, you create a new web service and connect it to the code repository on GitHub.

Then configure the service and set the environment variables.

Now your service is ready to use and you will receive an online URL for the service, which will be the apiUrl for the frontend application.

If you later make changes to the backend project and post them to the remote GitHub repository, the service will automatically go online without you having to take any further steps.

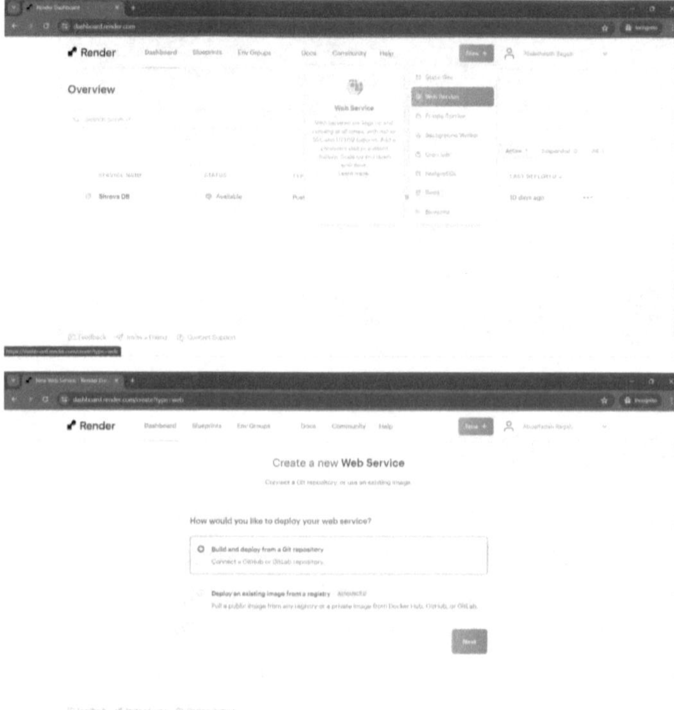

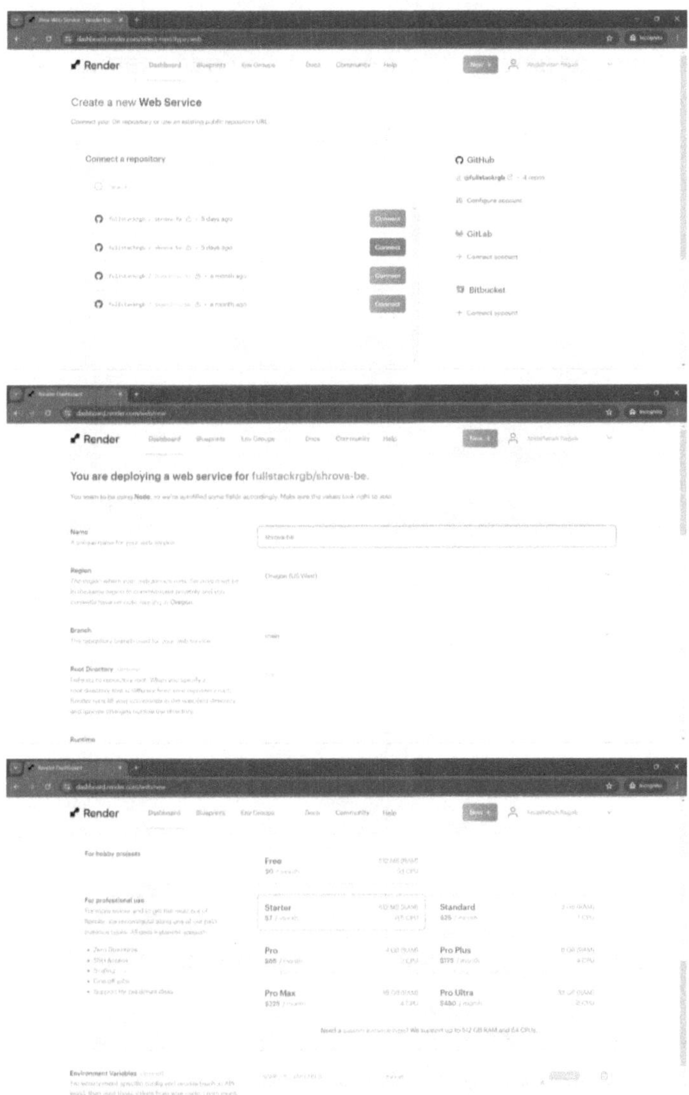

Choose one of the professional packages, you can start with the starter package and upgrade later.

Add environment variables. You can add them individually or select "Add from .env" to add them all at once.

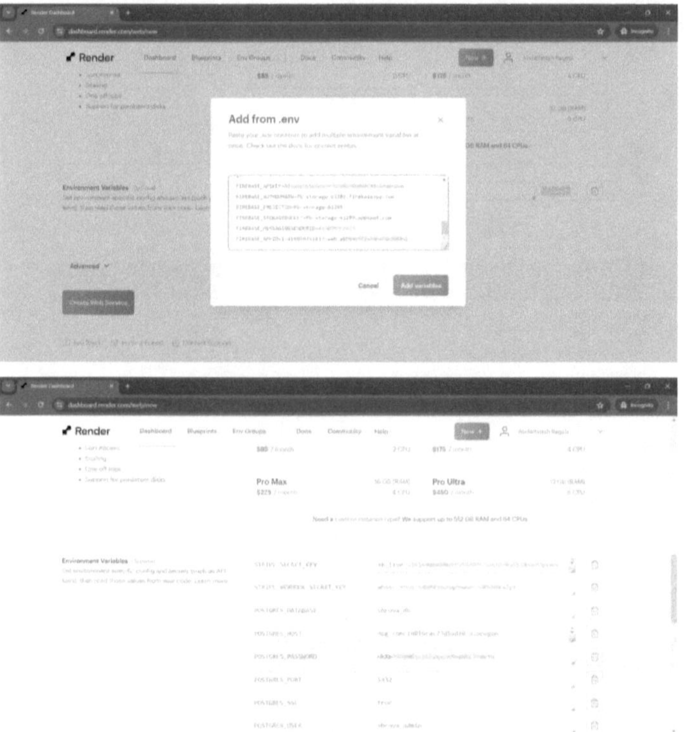

Some environment variables must be changed online from the local computer:

- STRIPE_SECRET_KEY: use the **live keys** and not the test keys.
- STRIPE_WEBHOOK_SECRET_KEY: use the **live keys** and not the test keys.

- POSTGRES_HOST: use the **short hostname** and not the long one, as all communication is handled internally within the render.com network.
- POSTGRES_SSL: set to **false** because all communication is handled internally within the render.com network.
- SHIPPO_TOKEN: use the **live token** and not the test token

Your backend application is automatically deployed and you now have the online URL that you will later use for the frontend application.

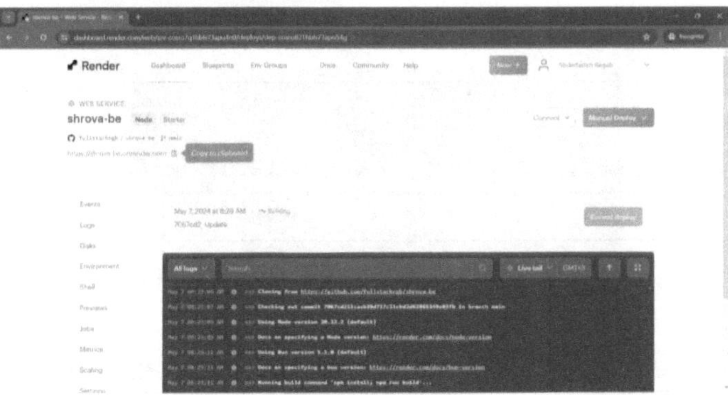

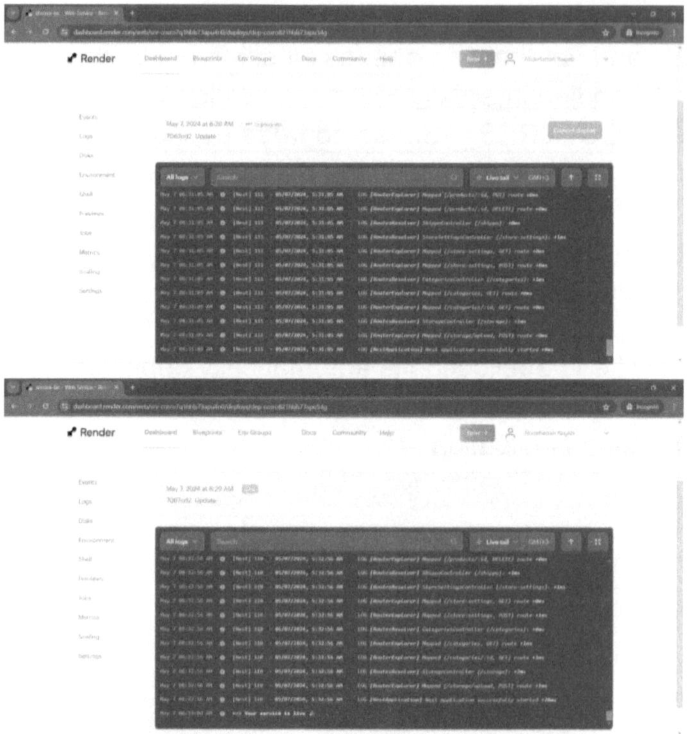

Now we are finished with the backend application and come to the last part, the frontend application.

Prepare your machine

If you are using Angular on your computer for the first time, you need to install it first.
To install Angular, follow these steps:

- Download NodeJS and install it
- Run the command `npm install -g @angular/cli`

Create new project

Create the angular project **shrova-fe** on your local machine as follows, execute the command

`ng new shrova-fe`

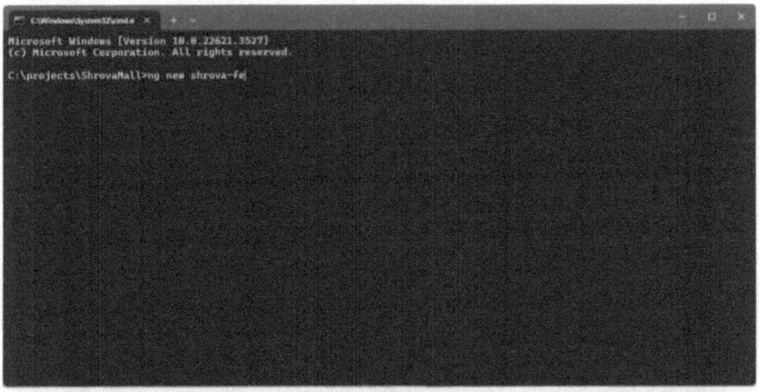

```
C:\Windows\System32\cmd.e    ×    +  ∨                          −  □  ×

Microsoft Windows [Version 10.0.22621.3527]
(c) Microsoft Corporation. All rights reserved.

C:\projects\ShrovaMall>ng new shrova-fe
```

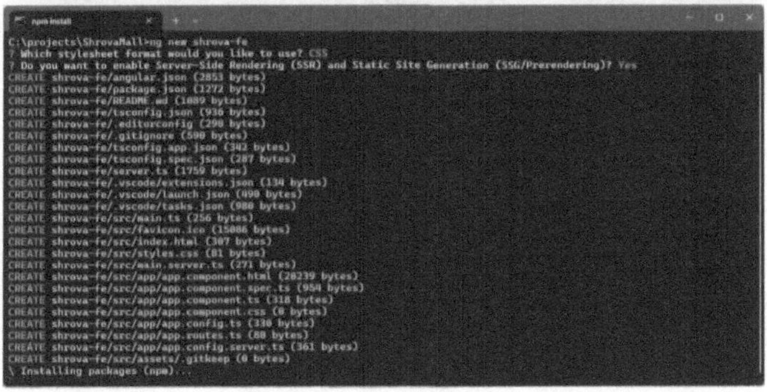

```
npm install                  ×    +  ∨                          −  □  ×

C:\projects\ShrovaMall>ng new shrova-fe
? Which stylesheet format would you like to use? CSS
? Do you want to enable Server-Side Rendering (SSR) and Static Site Generation (SSG/Prerendering)? Yes
CREATE shrova-fe/angular.json (2853 bytes)
CREATE shrova-fe/package.json (1272 bytes)
CREATE shrova-fe/README.md (1089 bytes)
CREATE shrova-fe/tsconfig.json (936 bytes)
CREATE shrova-fe/.editorconfig (298 bytes)
CREATE shrova-fe/.gitignore (590 bytes)
CREATE shrova-fe/tsconfig.app.json (302 bytes)
CREATE shrova-fe/tsconfig.spec.json (287 bytes)
CREATE shrova-fe/server.ts (1759 bytes)
CREATE shrova-fe/.vscode/extensions.json (134 bytes)
CREATE shrova-fe/.vscode/launch.json (490 bytes)
CREATE shrova-fe/.vscode/tasks.json (980 bytes)
CREATE shrova-fe/src/main.ts (256 bytes)
CREATE shrova-fe/src/favicon.ico (15086 bytes)
CREATE shrova-fe/src/index.html (307 bytes)
CREATE shrova-fe/src/styles.css (81 bytes)
CREATE shrova-fe/src/main.server.ts (271 bytes)
CREATE shrova-fe/src/app/app.component.html (20239 bytes)
CREATE shrova-fe/src/app/app.component.spec.ts (954 bytes)
CREATE shrova-fe/src/app/app.component.ts (318 bytes)
CREATE shrova-fe/src/app/app.component.css (0 bytes)
CREATE shrova-fe/src/app/app.config.ts (330 bytes)
CREATE shrova-fe/src/app/app.routes.ts (80 bytes)
CREATE shrova-fe/src/app/app.config.server.ts (361 bytes)
CREATE shrova-fe/src/assets/.gitkeep (0 bytes)
\ Installing packages (npm)...
```

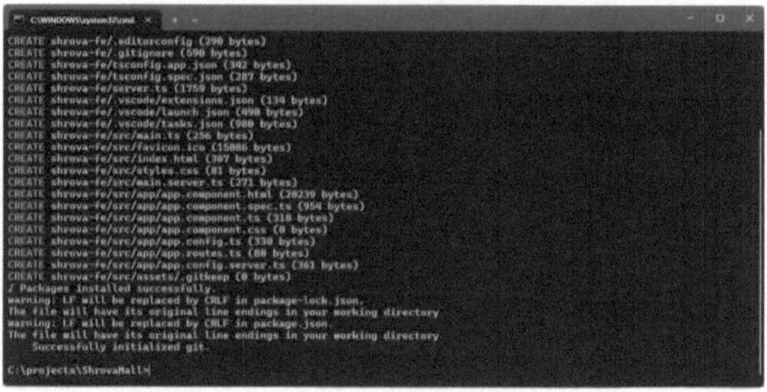

Select "Open folder..." in the file menu or on the start screen", navigate to the project folder and open it.

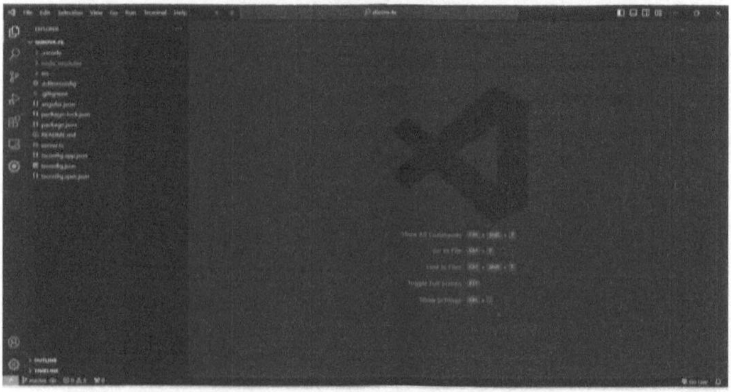

GitHub

Create a new repository **shrova-fe** for the frontend project as follows

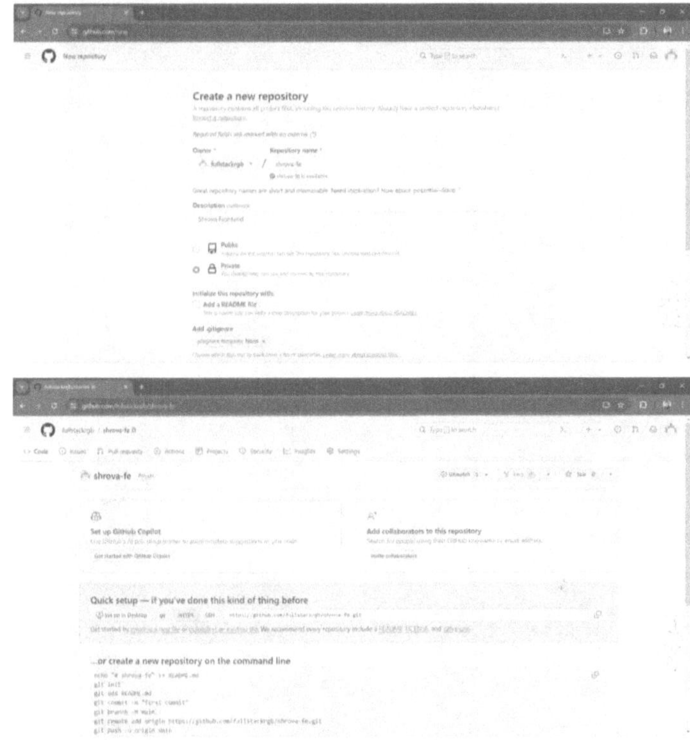

Connect to GitHub

Open the Visual Studio Code terminal

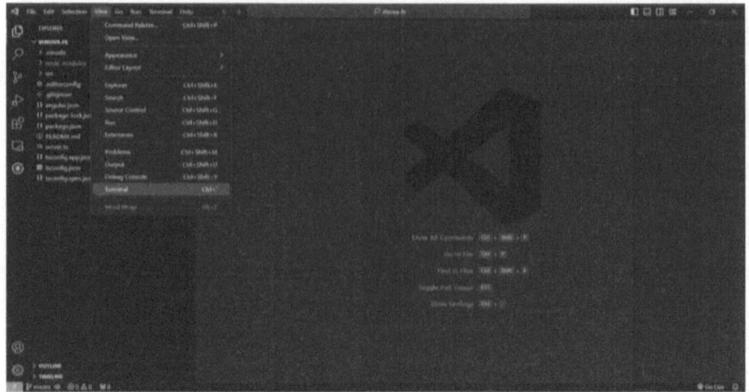

Execute the commands:

```
git add .
```

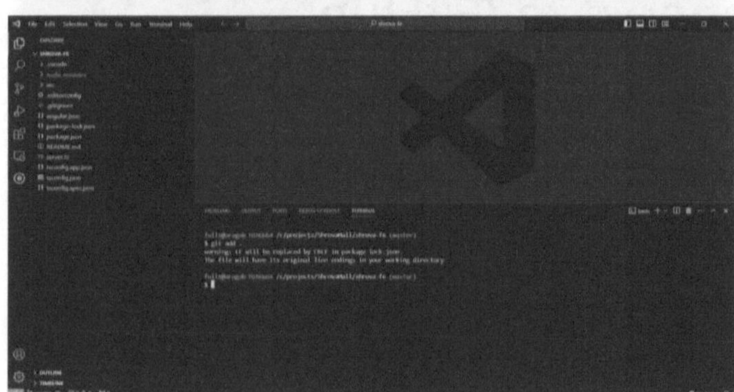

git commit -m "Initial"

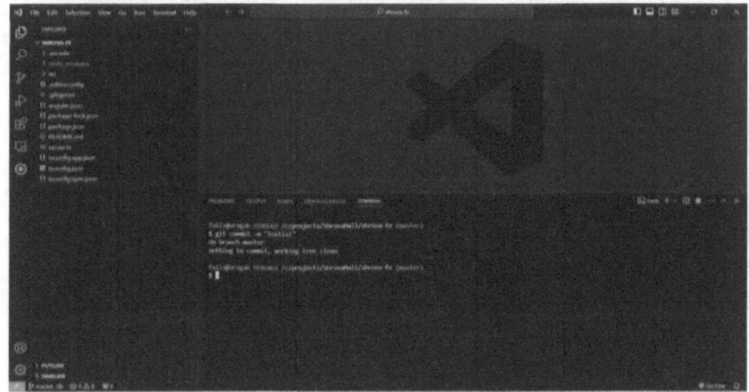

git branch -M main

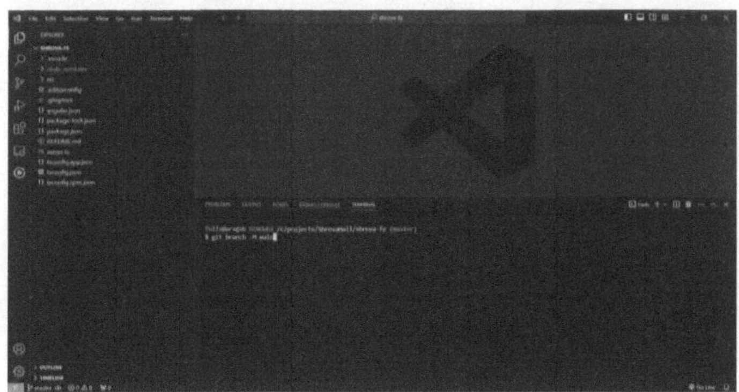

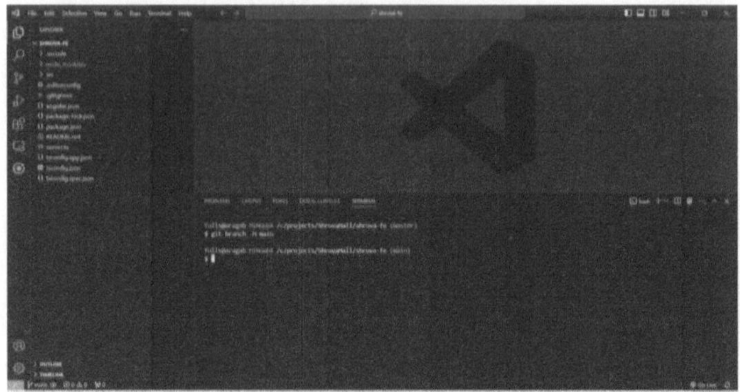

```
git remote add origin
https://ghp_uO5UWwrJ6P91gOK4PaTcSdvoIIDmfo2XOjX
5@github.com/fullstackrgb/shrova-fe.git
```

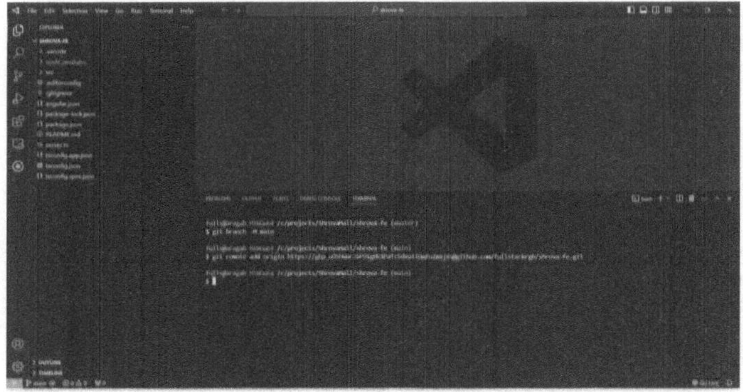

Note: I use a Personal Access Token to connect to GitHub.

```
git push -u origin main
```

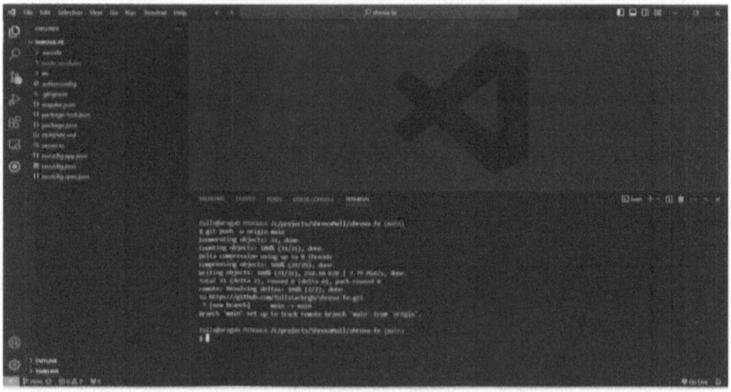

Note: To clear the terminal use the command `clear` *for Git Bash and* `cls` *for the Command Prompt*

When you want to push modifications online, you can execute the commands:
```
git add .
git commit -m "update message"
git push
```

Install Dependencies

We will use the following dependencies, so install them
- @stripe/stripe-js
- ngx-quill
- primeicons
- primeng

```
npm install @stripe/stripe-js express ngx-quill
primeicons primeng
```

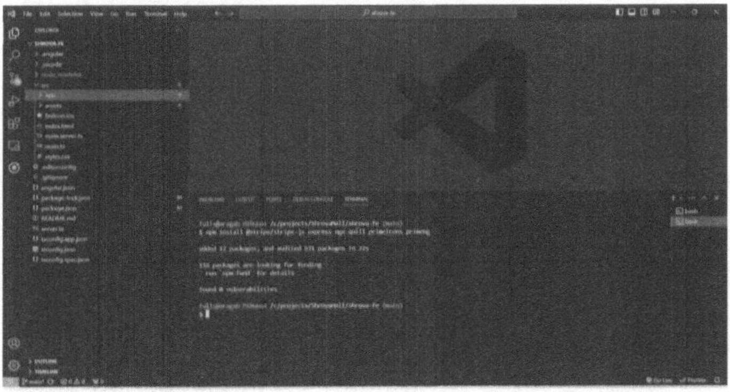

SEO

All Angular applications now have SSR enabled by default. Let's add some SEO details to our Angular application.

Insert the following tags within the <head> tag in the **index.html** file:

* <meta charset="utf-8" />
* <title>Shrova Mall</title>
* <base href="/" />
* <meta name="description" content="Online Ecommerce Store." />
* <meta name="keywords" content="shrova mall, online ecommerce store, shop online, buy products, online shopping" />
* <meta name="author" content="Shrova Mall" />
* <meta name="viewport" content="width=device-width, initial-scale=1" />
* <meta name="robots" content="index, follow" />

- `<link rel="canonical" href="https://shrovamall.com" />`
- `<link rel="icon" type="image/png" href="assets/images/logo.png" />`
- `<meta property="og:title" content="Shrova Mall" />`
- `<meta property="og:description" content="Online Ecommerce Store" />`
- `<meta property="og:image" content="https://shrovamall.com/assets/images/logo.png" />`
- `<meta property="og:url" content="https://shrovamall.com" />`
- `<meta property="og:type" content="website" />`

Code organization

As I work on the code, I will create many different artifacts and place them in different folders depending on their function.

So we have the following folders:

- components: small components
- data: data models and constants
- directives
- guards
- interceptors
- layout: layout components such as top bar, sidenav and footer
- pages: pages of the application such as Home, About, product detail page and so on

- pipes
- policies: pages for policy pages such as privacy policy, terms and conditions and so on
- services

First pages

Create two new pages, one for the homepage and one for not found.

The content of the homepage is still empty at the moment, but soon we will fill it with content. For the "Not found" page, I'll add a message saying that the requested page was not found or 404.

Routing

The default route has an empty path. So if the path is empty, I will redirect to "home". And I set "home" to load the HomeComponent.

For "not found" I set the placeholder "**" to redirect to "not found" and set "not found" to load the component "not found". This is what it looks like:

```
  { path: '', redirectTo: 'home', pathMatch:
'full' },
  { path: 'home', component: HomeComponent },
  ...
  { path: 'not-found', component:
NotFoundComponent },
  { path: '**', redirectTo: 'not-found' },
```

Layout components

Now I create the layout components, the top bar, the sidenav and the footer and will use them as follows. Angular loads the content of the current page into the Router Outlet component.
I add the top bar component before the router outlet and use CSS to display it at the top of the website.
For the sidebar, I'll also use CSS styles to place it at the edge of the page.
Finally, I'll add the footer after the router outlet and use CSS styles to display it at the bottom of the page. Like this:

```
<app-top-bar></app-top-bar>
<app-sidenav></app-sidenav>
<router-outlet />
<app-footer></app-footer>
```

Static pages

You can start by creating static pages with fixed content, such as "About us", "Contact", policies like "Privacy policy" and so on.

To create a new Angular component, execute the command `ng g c pages/pageName`

Pages are components, but they are associated with routes. So for each page I create, I add a new entry in the routes configuration file

Environments

You can generate environments by executing the command `ng generate environments`

Add the following keys to the two environment files

```
export const environment = {
  API_URL: 'http://localhost:3000',
  STRIPE_PK:
'pk_test_51K1KB...USE_YOUR_STRIPE_TEST_KEY',
};
```

When we are ready for production, we will use the live keys for Stripe and the backend

Main folders

components

Contains components that are used in our Angular application

data

Contains data models and constants that are used in our Angular application.

directives

Contains directives that are used in our Angular application

guards

Contains guards that are used in our Angular application

interceptors

Contains interceptors that are used in our Angular application

layout

Contains layout components of top-bar, sidenav and footer that are used in our Angular application

pages

Contains pages that are used in our application

pipes

Contains pipes that are used in our Angular application

policies

Contains policy pages that are used in our application

services

Contains services that are used in our application

Common scenarios

The code is available for you to download and you can view it yourself. Trying to explain all the components here would take too much time, because you can understand everything in a few seconds by looking at the code. Therefore, I will focus on some common scenarios and explain how I built them.

Auth area

The login pages are the registration page, the login page, the "Forgot password" page and the "New password" page.
I created the authService to connect to the backend auth module and manage all auth operations.

The register page is just a component that is connected to a route.
To create the component, execute the command
ng g c pages/signup

Insert a new entry in the route array.

On the signup page, I create a form with the basic details of first name, last name, email and password.

The submit button sends this data to the backend service and updates the frontend with the result. The page is redirected to the start page.

The same is for the login page.

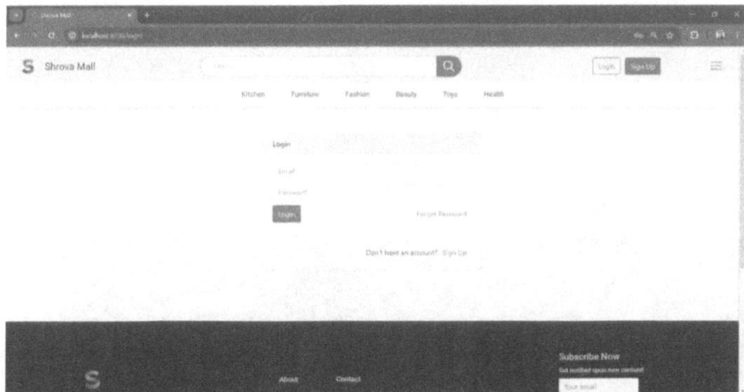

Two other pages I have created are the "Forgot password" and "New password" pages.
It's very simple: the user enters their email address and sends it to the backend. They are then redirected to the "New password" page where they can enter a new password.

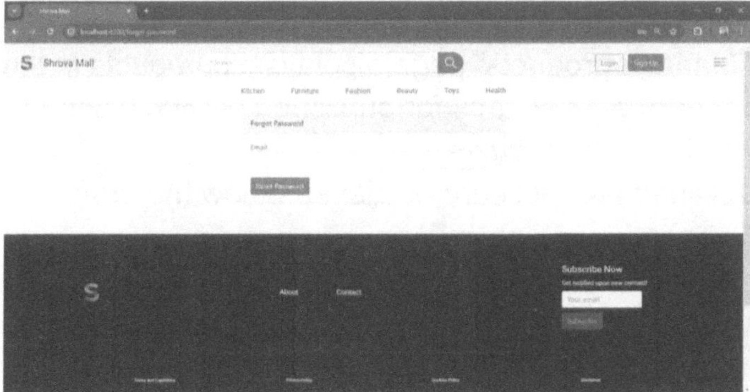

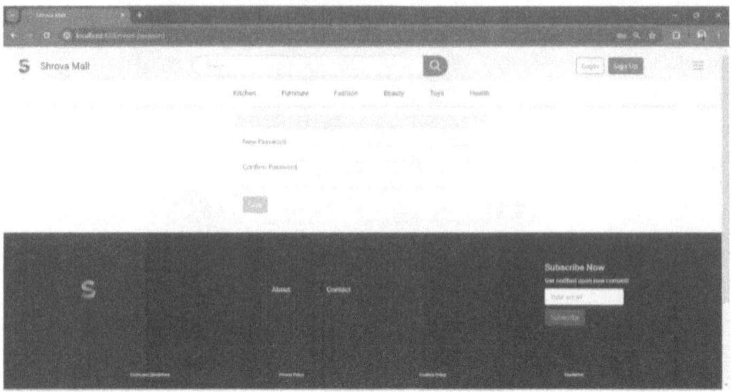

Admin area

We need the admin area to add products to the app.
For our store to work, we need three administration
pages: the Manage products page, the Add new product
page and the Store settings page.
The "Manage products" page displays all products in the
store. There are two tabs for published products and
another for draft products.
Unpublished products are displayed below the draft
area.

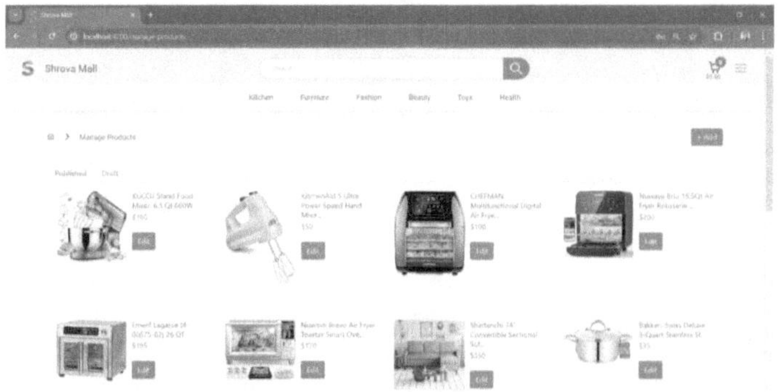

The "Add products" page consists of a large form with many fields in which the product details can be entered. We use Primeng controls throughout the system, including for the file upload controls. We use Firebase Storage to store the selected file image online in Firebase Storage.

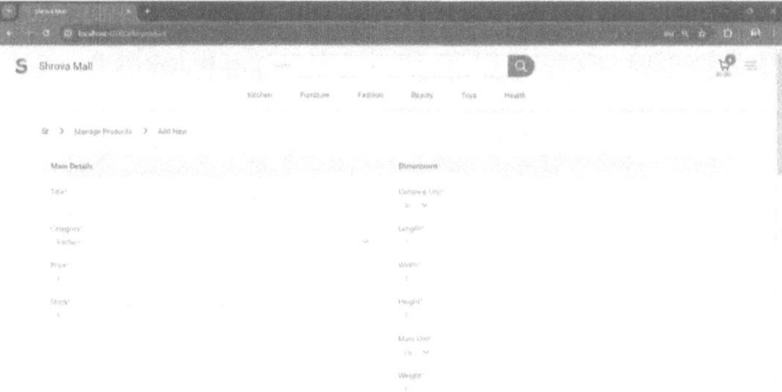

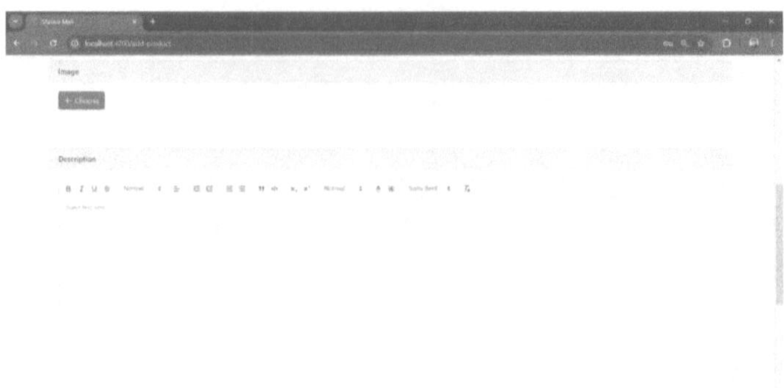

For the description I use the quill-editor from the
ngx-quill package and I use the quill-view-html from the
same package on the product detail page to display the
product description.

For the store settings page, I created a form to save all
the page details. All fields must be filled in as they will
be used as the brand name and will be used when
shipping products to customers.

Homepage

First we have the "featured products" or "featured deals".
Below I show some products.

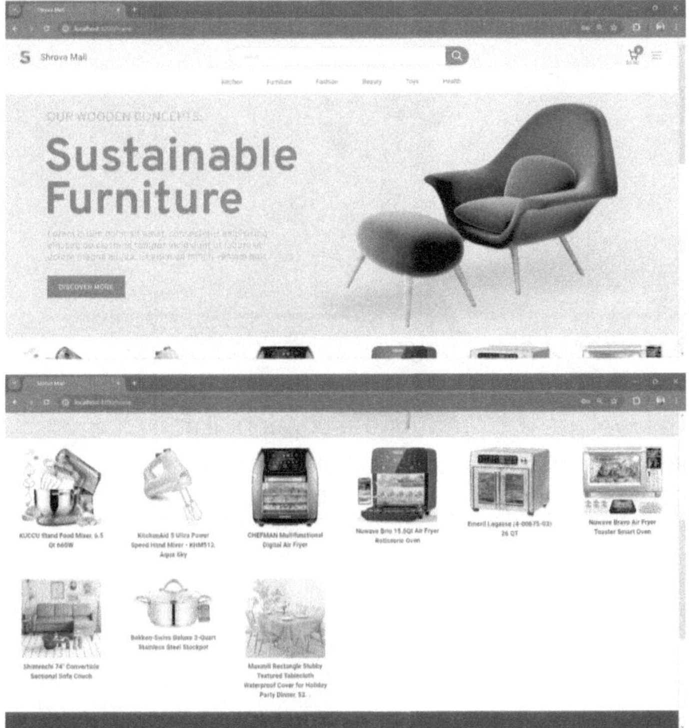

For the sake of simplicity, I use a picture for the "featured products" section.

Product details

If you click on the product card, you will be redirected to the product detail page.

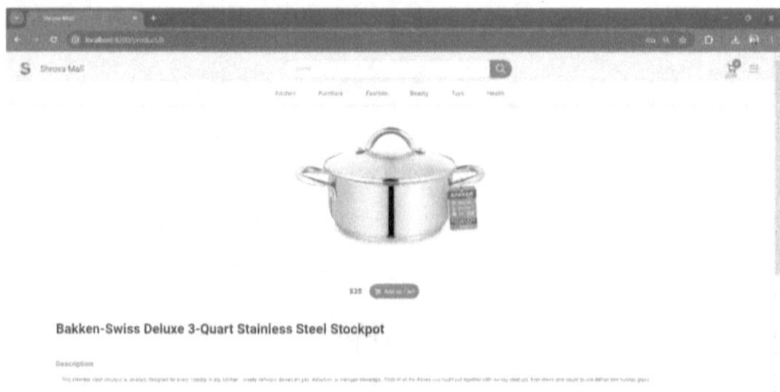

On the product detail page you will find the image, the price and a button to add the product to the shopping cart, as well as the product description. Each click on the add button adds another item to the shopping cart.

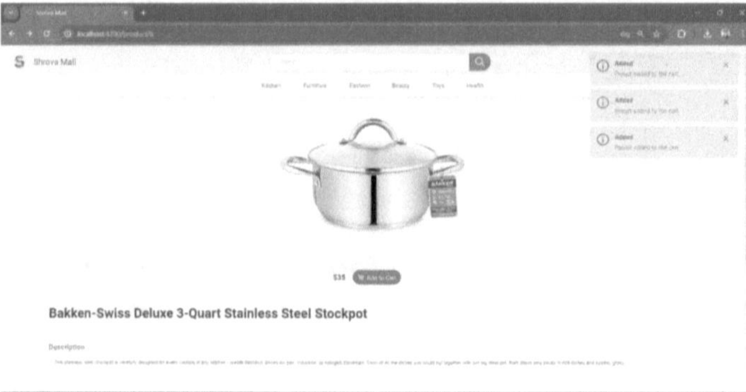

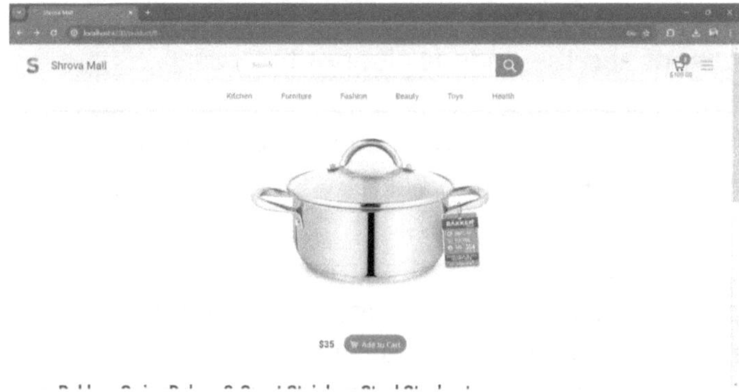

Shopping cart

If you click on the shopping cart icon at the top right, you will be redirected to the shopping cart page

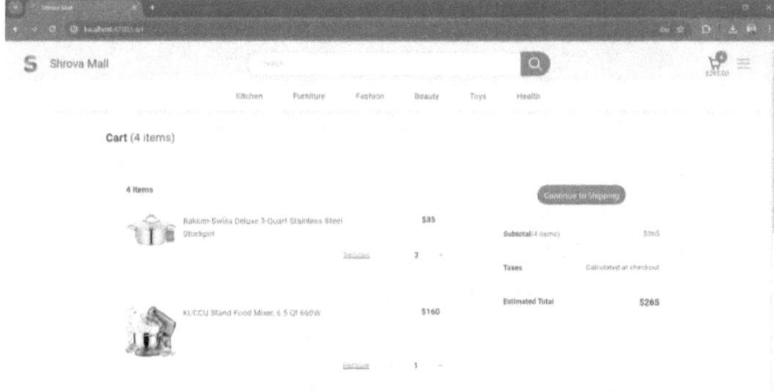

The shopping cart page has two main components, one for the items and one for the summary.

I created a component called "cart-item-card" that accepts cartItem as input and displays it on the screen.

Now it's easier to loop over the cart-item-card component and the code is cleaner too.

On the other side, the total price is displayed in the summary on the right-hand side.

The page is responsive and on mobile the two components are arranged vertically one behind the other, while on desktop they are next to each other.

All pages in our application are fully responsive.

Shipping

The next step after the shopping cart is shipping. First enter the destination address and select the shipping rate.
The shipping rates are calculated on the basis of the addressFrom, the addressTo and the parcels. The From address is the address of the store that you specified on the store settings page. The addressTo is the destination address that the customer enters on the shipping page. The parcels are the products to be shipped, with each product having its own dimensions.
I send all this information to shippo and it provides a list of rates that I show to the user on the page. The customer then select the appropriate shipping option and I add it to the order summary. I use this information to calculate the total amount of the order by adding the shipping costs to the order total, and to later receive the

shipping label after the order has been successfully completed.

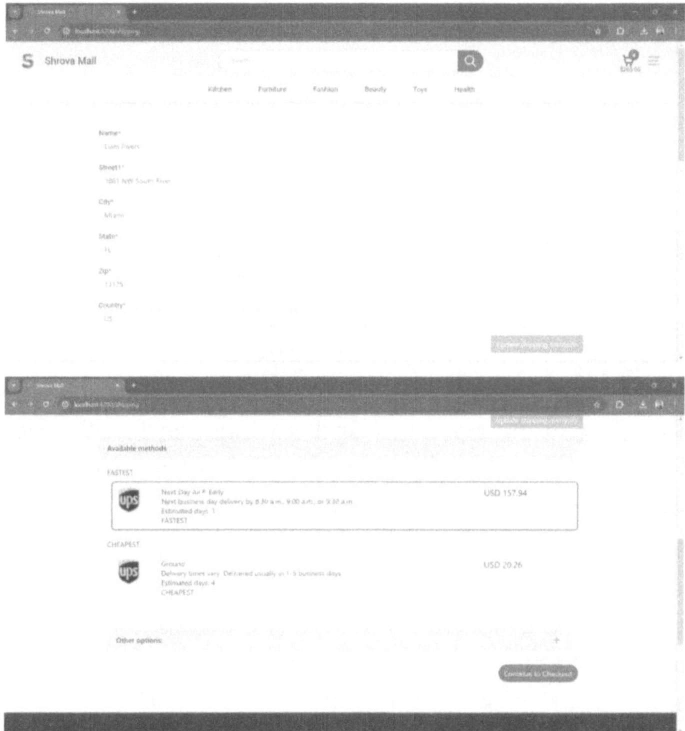

Checkout

The last step before payment is to check the order summary. Here you will find a list of all items ordered with their quantities and total prices.
The subtotal, the shipping costs and the total amount are also displayed.

Payment

The last step is the payment and is processed by Stripe. I transfer all order data to Stripe and it collects the money from the customer to my Stripe account.
Once the payment is successfully completed, I receive an event confirming the successful payment. I then add the order to the database and ship the product to the customer. The customer is redirected to the success page, which informs them that their order was successful and they can track it on the order page.
Since the shipping service providers provide us with tracking numbers and tracking urls, which I attach to the order record before saving it in the database, users can use them to track the delivery with the respective provider at any time.

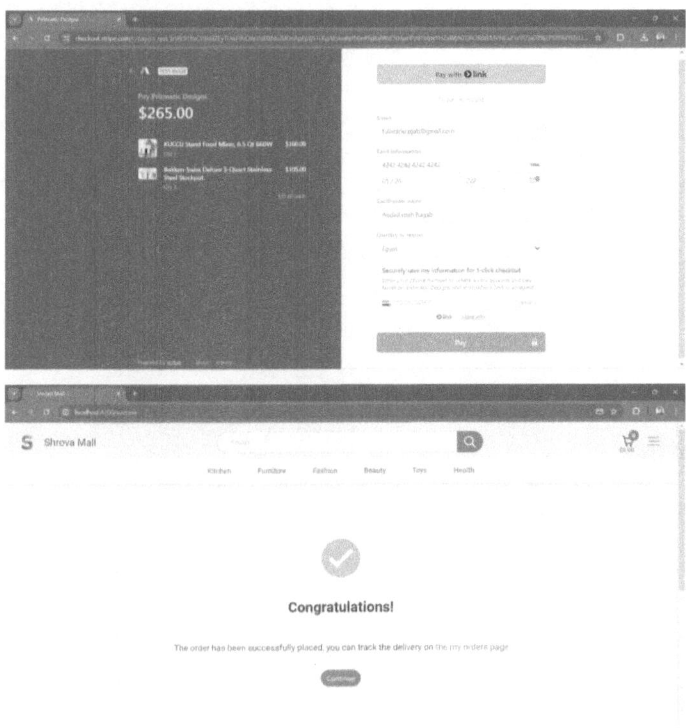

My orders

On the "My orders" page, you can view a summary of your order at any time and track the delivery of your order.

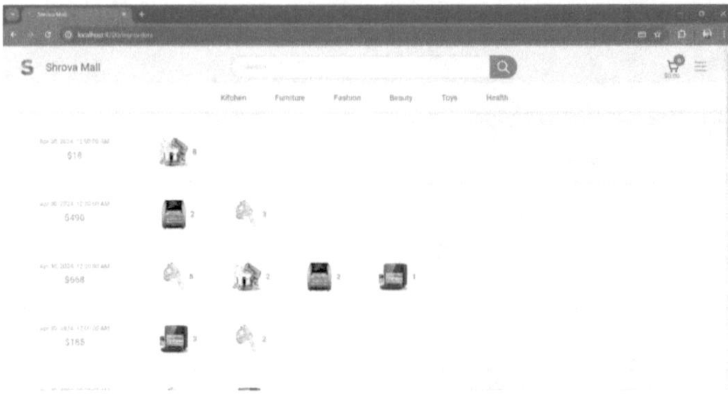

profile

Users can update their profile data on the profile page.

The second important point on the profile page is the

"Address" tab, where users can enter their addresses

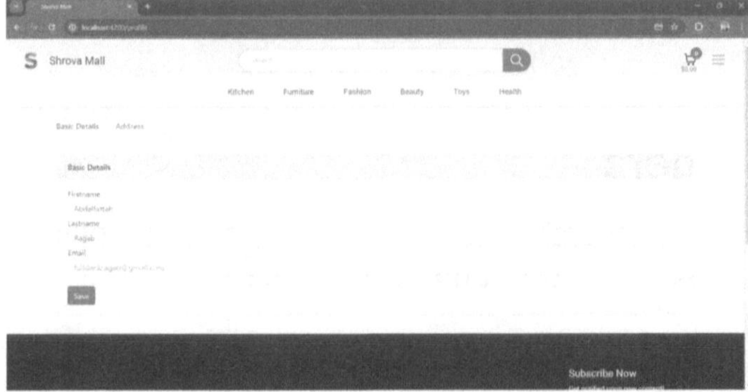

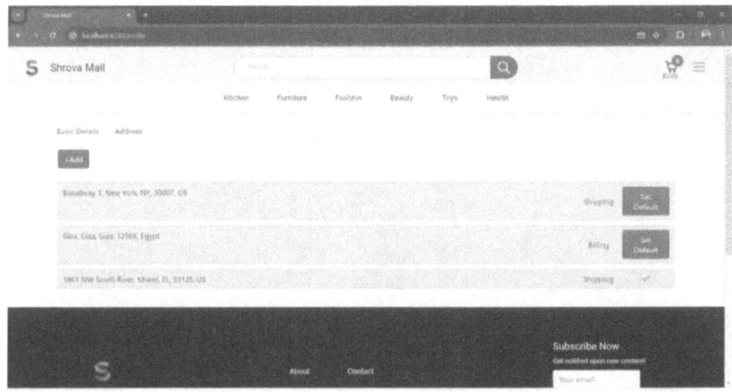

Deployment

To deploy your application to Render.com, create a new static website. You will be prompted to select the GitHub repository of your project. After selecting it, you will be prompted to make some settings.

Leave everything unchanged, but set the "Publishing directory" to "dist/shrova-fe/browser"

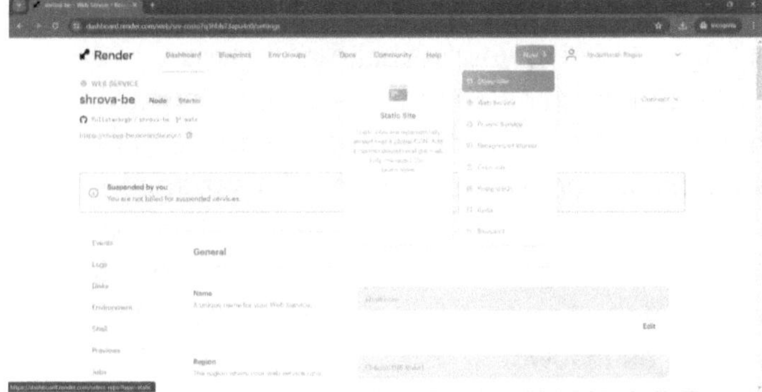

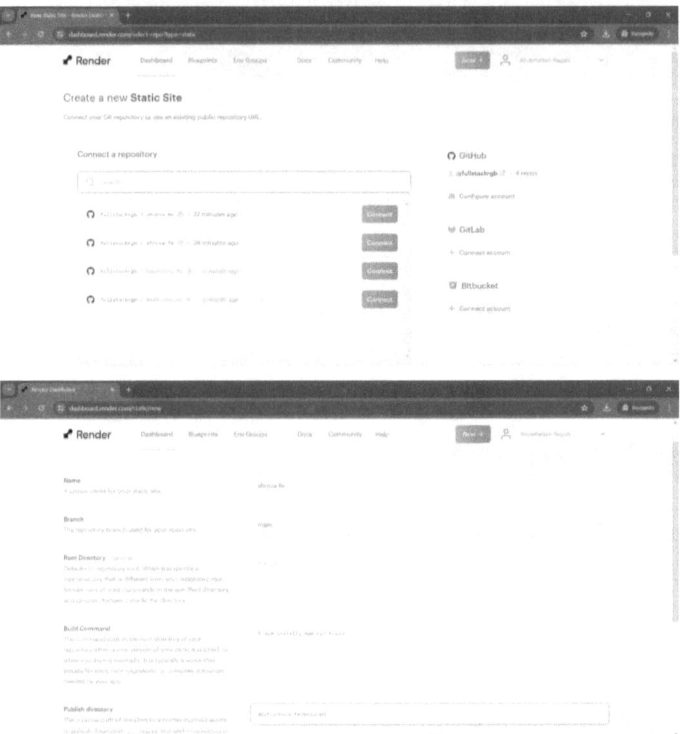

It then starts building your website and gives you a url for your website online. On the Redirects/Rewrites tab, you need to add a rule that is important for Angular applications to work properly online. This is important if the user refreshes the website or wants to land on a specific internal page and not on the homepage. To make the Angular router work properly, I will set a rewrite rule as follows:

Source: **/***

Destination: **/index.html**

Action: **Rewrite**

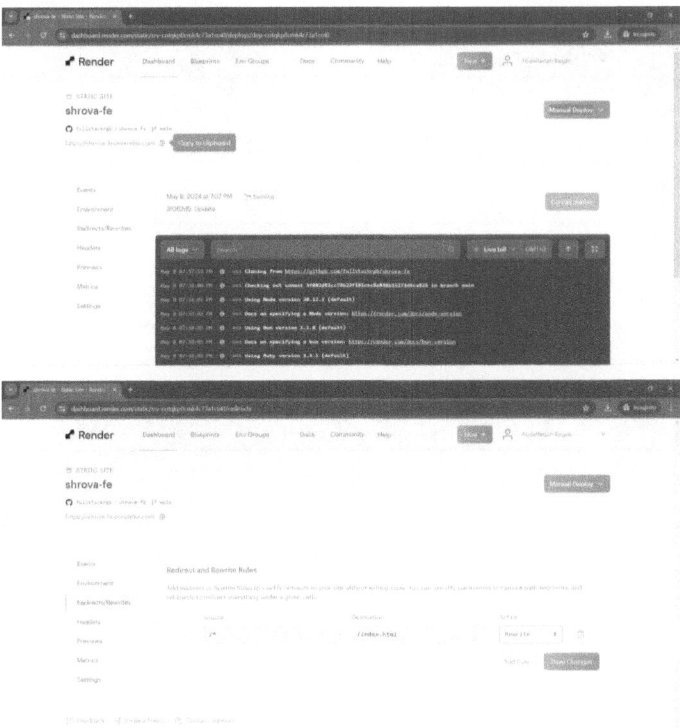

The last setting is to connect your application to a custom domain like shrovamall.com. Scroll down the settings page until you reach the "Custom domains" section.

Before adding your custom domain here, you'll need to update its DNS by adding a new CNAME record that points to the URL on render.com. Go to your domain provider and add a new CNAME record pointing to render.

Go back to the render settings, click on the "Add custom domain" button and add your new custom domain.

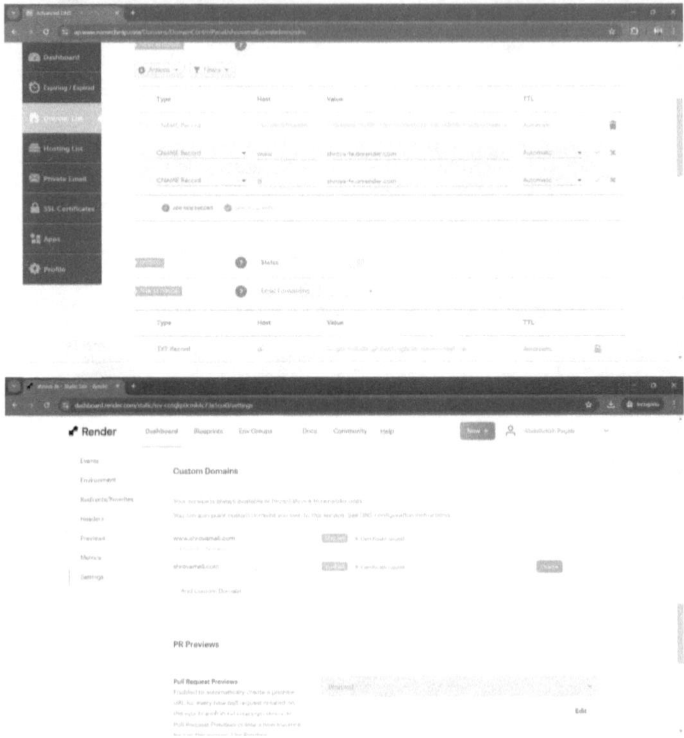

Congratulations, your store is now up and running!

Conclusion

Congratulations! You have completed the book "Shrova Mall: A-to-Z e-commerce full-stack application". Now you have your online business up and running. Remember that learning is an ongoing process. Practice makes perfect — create your own projects, experiment with the features you have learned, and delve into the extensive online resources.

Thank you for joining me in my exploration of the complete e-commerce application. I wish you the best of luck on your programming journey.

Media Attribution

Women buying clothes in apparel store. dress, lady, accessory flat vector illustration. fashion and shopping
Image by pch.vector on Freepik

E commerce landing page
Image by freepik

Logo template design
Image by flatart on Freepik

Don't miss out!

Receive an email when Abdelfattah Ragab publishes a new book. It's free and without obligation.

Also by Abdelfattah Ragab

◇ Angular Generative AI

◇ Angular Performance Optimization

◇ Angular Reactive Forms

◇ Angular Observables and Promises

◇ Angular HTTP

◇ React Portfolio App Development

About the Author

Abdelfattah Ragab is a professional software developer
with more than 20 years of experience.
https://abdelfattah-ragab.com

About the Publisher

Abdelfattah Ragab is a highly qualified and experienced software developer with over 20 years of experience in the industry. Specializing in front-end development, Abdelfattah Ragab has a deep understanding of Angular, JavaScript, TypeScript, HTML and CSS. Read more at https://abdelfattah-ragab.com

www.ingramcontent.com/pod-product-compliance
Lightning Source LLC
La Vergne TN
LVHW040517200726
843493LV00017B/1318